BK-323

122 Fold and Say® Auditory & Story Comprehension Activity Booklets

Listening and Reading Comprehension!

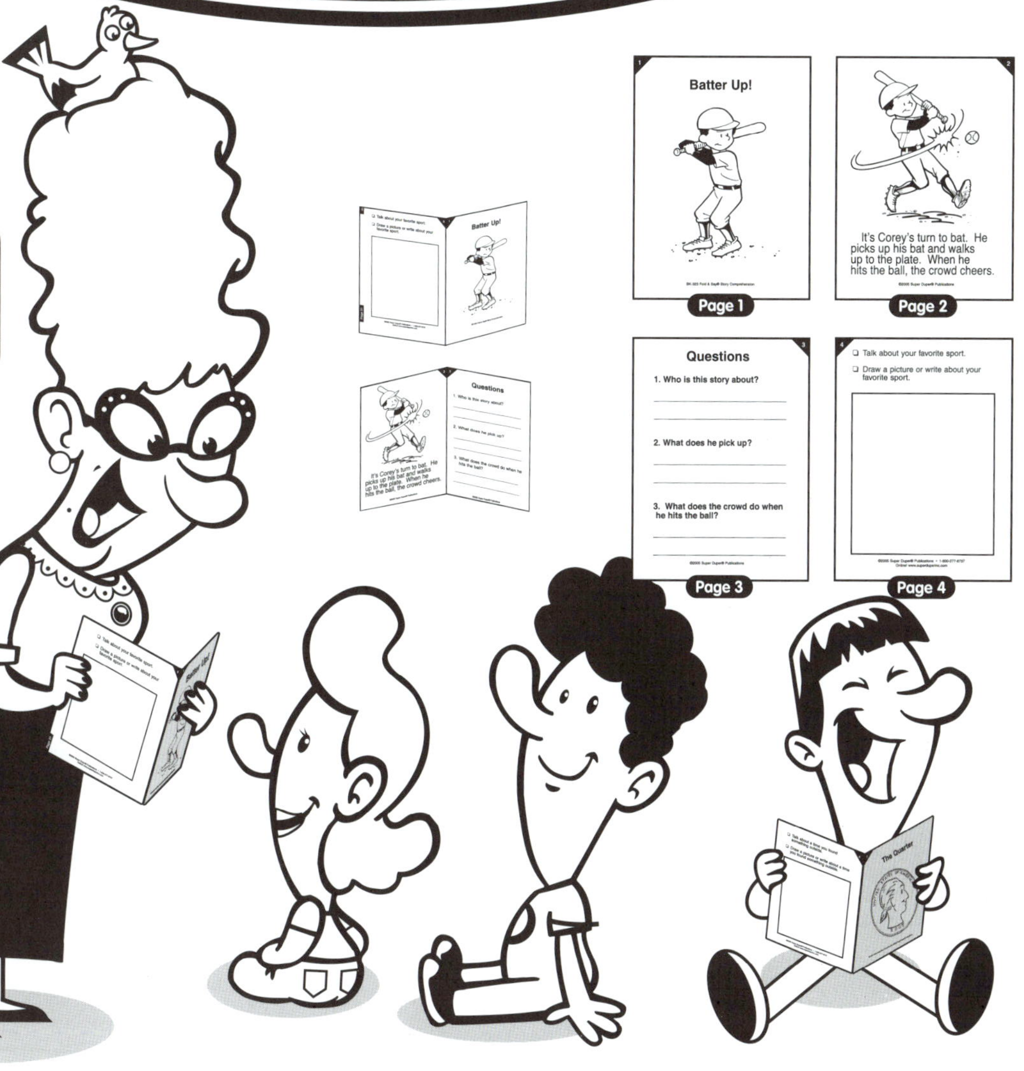

Batter Up!

It's Corey's turn to bat. He picks up his bat and walks up to the plate. When he hits the ball, the crowd cheers.

Questions

1. Who is this story about?

2. What does he pick up?

3. What does the crowd do when he hits the ball?

❑ Talk about your favorite sport.

❑ Draw a picture or write about your favorite sport.

Page 1 Page 2 Page 3 Page 4

Written by Diane Hyde, M. Ed.
Edited by Lisa Pridy
Illustrated by Ted Dawson & Ryan Bradburn

Post Office Box 24997, Greenville, South Carolina 29616
Call 1-800-277-8737 • Fax 1-800-978-7379
Online! www.superduperinc.com
E-Mail: custserv@superduperinc.com

ISBN 1-58650-572-6

Dedication

To my wonderful husband, who stands beside me and encourages me. He stands beside me when I get frustrated and puts up with my desire to write, even though at times he is “jealous” of the computer taking up our time together. One could not ask for a better partner in life.

Diane

Introduction

122 Fold and Say® Auditory & Story Comprehension contains 122 short stories to improve students' reading comprehension, listening comprehension, and reasoning skills. The stories have two levels: *Level One* for beginners and *Level Two* for advanced practice. Copy each page and fold into a 4-page booklet. *Auditory & Story Comprehension* also includes a parent letter and three award certificates, plus a bonus CD-ROM with the same black and white pages as the book, so you can print these pages from your computer.

Level One contains 61, three-sentence short stories. Students listen to the story as a helper reads it, or they read it themselves. Then, they answer three story comprehension questions, and talk, draw, or write about a common situation related to the story.

Level Two contains 61, four-sentence short stories. Students listen to/read the story, and then select the main idea of the story from a choice of three answers. (An answer key is in the back of the book.) Three story comprehension questions follow. The extension activities give students a creative way to talk, draw, or write about a situation related to the story.

Table of Contents

Table of Contents

Parent/Caregiver Letter

Date:____________________

Dear Parent or Caregiver,

In _________________________________ class, your child is improving his/her ability to listen to/read a story and answer main idea and/or story comprehension questions. You can help your child improve these skills by completing the attached activities.

Please complete the activities checked below:

- ❑ Read the story aloud to your child. Then, have him/her answer aloud the story comprehension questions on page 3.
- ❑ Have your child listen to or read the story and answer the questions on page 2 and page 3.
- ❑ Have your child read the story aloud. Then, have him/her read and write down his/her answers to the story comprehension questions on page 3.
- ❑ Ask your child to talk about the activity on page 4.
- ❑ Ask your child to draw a picture or write down his/her response to the activity on page 4.
- ❑ For added practice, have your child retell the story.

____

____

____

Thank you for your help and support.

____

Name

Level 1 Stories

Jenna's Adventure

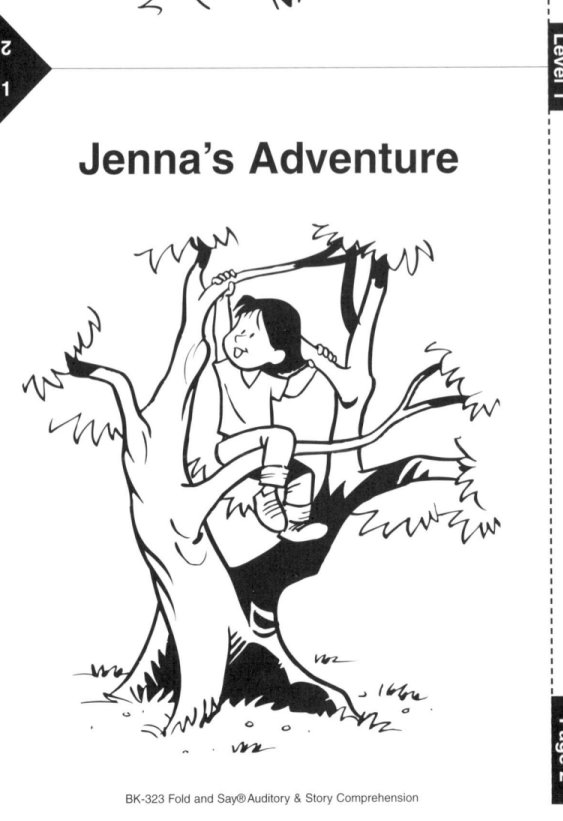

Jenna slowly climbs up the tree. Finally, she sits on a strong limb. She can see up and down the street.

Questions

1. Who climbs the tree?

2. Does she climb quickly or slowly?

3. What can she see from the tree?

- ❑ Talk about what happens next.
- ❑ Draw a picture or write about what happens next.

Cut on dotted line

Bennie Beaver's Home

Bennie Beaver is making a dam. He needs lots of wood to build the dam. Bennie stores food in the dam.

Questions

1. Who is this story about?

2. What does he need to build the dam?

3. Where does he store food?

❑ Talk about what your house looks like.

❑ Draw a picture or write about what your house looks like.

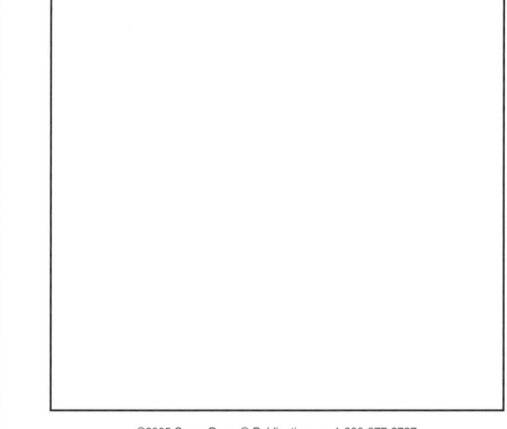

1 2 3 4

Cut on dotted line

Level 1

Leapfrog

Tommy Toad wants to play leapfrog. Along comes Sally Snail. She says, "I'll play leapfrog, Tommy."

Questions

1. What did Tommy want to play?

2. Who came along?

3. Is she going to play leapfrog with Tommy?

- ❑ Talk about a game you like to play.
- ❑ Draw a picture or write about a game you like to play.

Cartoons

Maria is watching cartoons. Her favorite cartoon is about horses. Mom makes popcorn for her while she watches.

Questions

1. Who is watching cartoons?

2. What is her favorite cartoon about?

3. What does her mom make for her?

❑ Talk about your favorite television show.

❑ Draw a picture or write about your favorite television show.

Hannah Hen

Hannah Hen walks to the store. Her chicks are behind her. If the chicks are good, Hannah will buy them candy.

Questions

1. Where is Hannah Hen walking?

2. Who walks behind her?

3. What will Hannah buy for her chicks if they are good?

- ❏ Talk about a time you went to the store with your parent or caregiver.
- ❏ Draw a picture or write about a time you went to the store with your parent or caregiver.

Pirate's Treasure

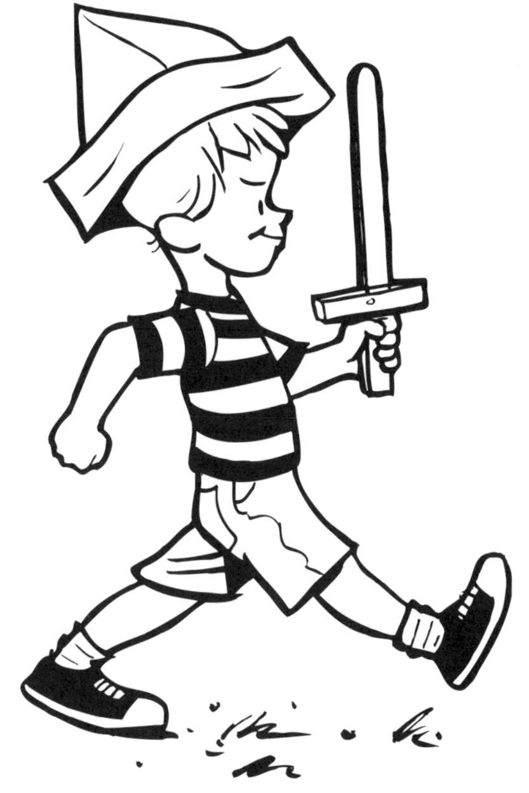

Ben is playing pirate. He uses a shovel to dig a hole. He is hunting for treasure.

Questions

1. Who is playing pirate?

____

____

2. What does he use to dig a hole?

____

____

3. What is he hunting for?

____

____

- ❑ Talk about what you think Ben might find.
- ❑ Draw a picture or write about what you think Ben might find.

Party Time

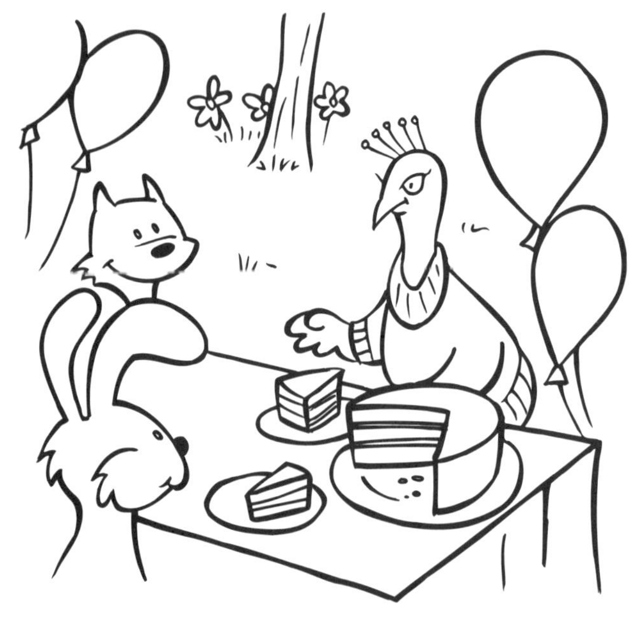

Patty Peacock goes to a party. The party is on the lake. She wears her new pink sweater.

Questions

1. Who is going to the party?

____

____

2. Where is the party?

____

____

3. What does she wear to the party?

____

____

- ❑ Talk about what you would wear to this party.
- ❑ Draw a picture or write about what you would wear to this party.

Farmer John

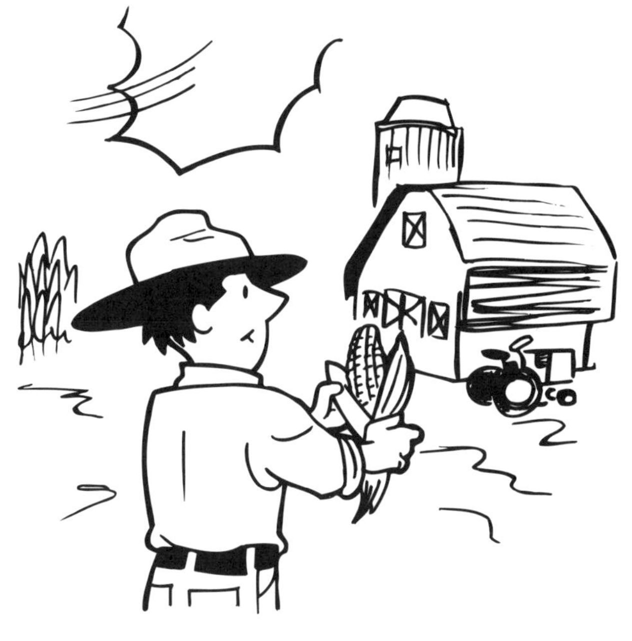

Farmer John lives on a farm. He grows corn and beans. He likes to ride his green tractor in the fields.

Questions

1. Where does Farmer John live?

2. What does he grow?

3. What color is his tractor?

- ❑ Talk about your favorite vegetable.
- ❑ Draw a picture or write about your favorite vegetable.

Zoo Trip

Luke goes to the zoo with his mom and dad. He wants to see the elephants. He feeds them peanuts.

Questions

1. Who goes to the zoo?

2. What does he want to see?

3. What does he feed them?

❏ Talk about your favorite zoo animal.

❏ Draw a picture or write about your favorite zoo animal.

Cut on dotted line

Balloons

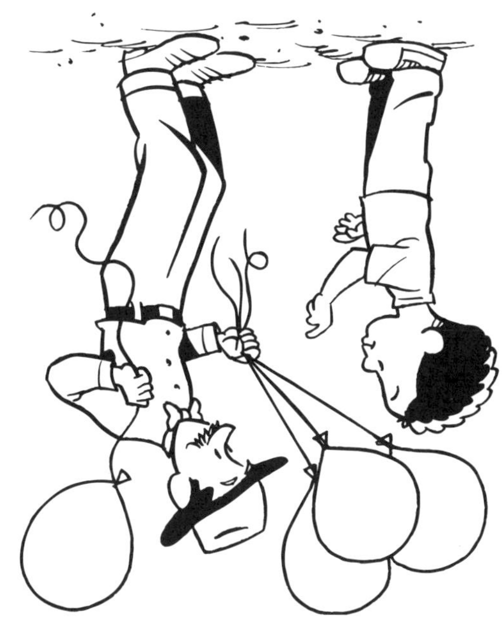

Jamie wants to buy a balloon. His dad gives him money. He buys a bright, yellow balloon.

Questions

1. Who wants to buy a balloon?

____

____

2. What does his dad give him?

____

____

3. What color balloon does he buy?

____

____

- ❏ Talk about your favorite color.
- ❏ Draw a picture or write about your favorite color.

Cut on dotted line

Level 1

Page 12

1 2
4 3

The Fair

Sam and Sue go to the fair.
They ride the Ferris wheel.
They like to eat cotton candy.

Questions

1. Who goes to the fair?

____

____

2. What do they ride?

____

____

3. What do they like to eat?

____

____

- ❑ Talk about what you would do at the fair.
- ❑ Draw a picture or write about what you would do at the fair.

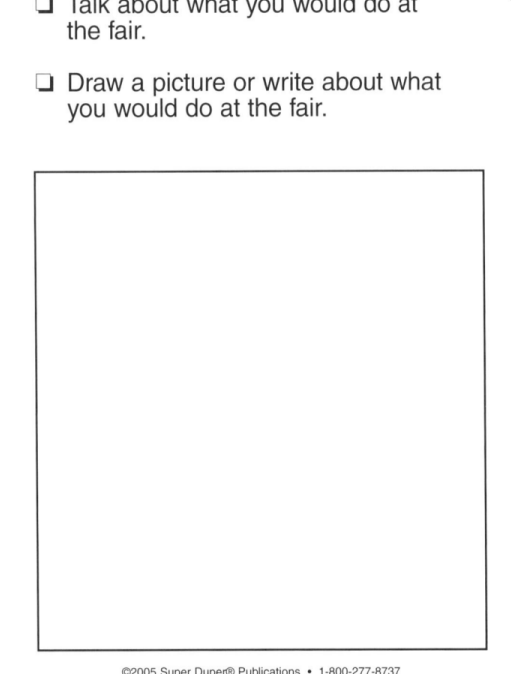

Brent the Cook

Brent is hungry. He cooks an egg in the skillet. He sits down to eat his breakfast.

Questions

1. Who is hungry?

2. What does he cook?

3. What meal is Brent eating?

- ❏ Talk about what you like to eat for breakfast.
- ❏ Draw a picture or write about what you like to eat for breakfast.

Car Wash

Mom's car is dirty. She washes the car. She dries the car with a towel.

Questions

1. Whose car is dirty?

2. What does she do?

3. What does she use to dry the car?

- ❏ Talk about how you would wash a car.
- ❏ Draw a picture or write about how you would wash a car.

Cut on dotted line

Fran's Fruit Stand

Fran grows fruit to sell. She grows oranges and apples. Each piece of fruit costs a quarter.

Questions

1. Who grows fruit?

____

____

2. What kind of fruit does she sell?

____

____

3. How much does a piece of fruit cost?

____

____

❏ Talk about your favorite fruit.

❏ Draw a picture or write about your favorite fruit.

Picnic

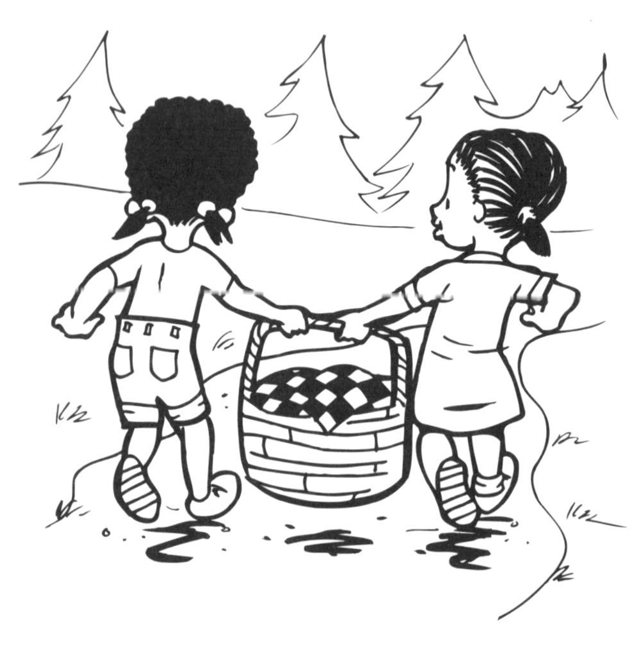

Jen and Lisa are having a picnic. They sit under the big tree. They eat sandwiches and cookies.

Questions

1. Who is having a picnic?

2. Where are they sitting?

3. What are they eating?

❏ Talk about what you like to eat on a picnic.

❏ Draw a picture or write about what you like to eat on a picnic.

Cut on dotted line

The Parade

Today is parade day. The band marches down the street. The clowns wave at the crowd.

Questions

1. When is the parade?

2. Who marches down the street?

3. Who waves at the crowd?

- ❑ Talk about what you like to see in a parade.
- ❑ Draw a picture or write about what you like to see in a parade.

Cut on dotted line

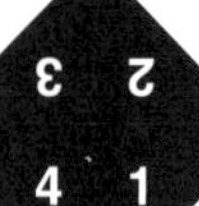

The Rainbow

Luis walks outside. He looks up at the sky. He sees a rainbow.

Questions

1. Who walks outside?

2. Where does he look?

3. What does he see?

- ❏ Talk about a rainbow you have seen.
- ❏ Draw a picture or write about a rainbow you have seen.

Cut on dotted line

Cut on dotted line

The Fishing Trip

Terry is fishing with her dad. She puts a worm on her pole. She wants to catch a big fish.

Questions

1. Who is fishing with Terry?

____

____

2. What does she put on her pole?

____

____

3. What does she want to catch?

____

____

- ❏ Talk about a type of fish you would want to catch on a fishing trip.
- ❏ Draw a picture or write about a type of fish you would want to catch on a fishing trip.

Mixed-Up Matt

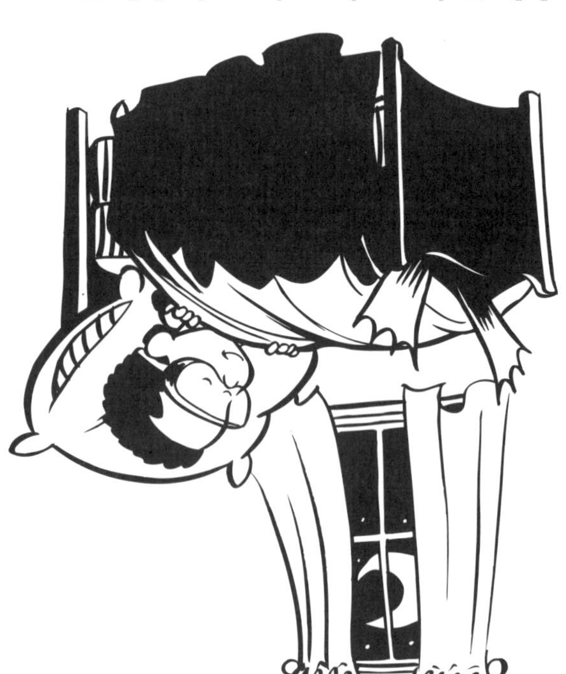

Matt is mixed up! Matt wears his goggles and fins to bed. He swims in his pajamas.

Questions

1. Who is this story about?

2. What does he wear to bed?

3. What does he swim in?

- ❏ Talk about a time you did something silly.
- ❏ Draw a picture or write about a time you did something silly.

Cut on dotted line

Splish, Splash

Austin fills the tub with soap and water. He puts his dog, Morgan, in the tub. Morgan splashes the water with her tail.

Questions

1. What does Austin fill the tub with?

2. What is the name of Austin's dog?

3. What does Morgan do with her tail?

- ❏ Talk about what happens next.
- ❏ Draw a picture or write about what happens next.

Cut on dotted line

Level 1

Bird Nest

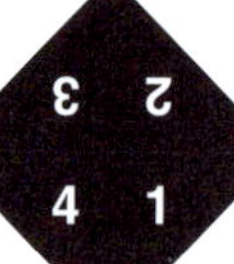

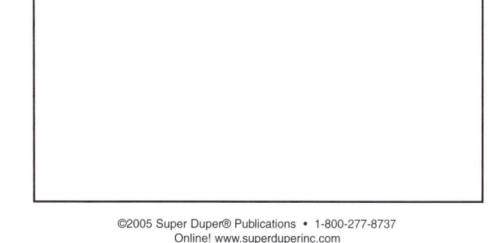

Chantal is sitting outside. She sees a nest in the dogwood tree. There is a blue bird in the nest.

Questions

1. Where is Chantal?

2. Where is the bird nest?

3. What color is the bird?

- ❏ Talk about a bird nest you have seen.
- ❏ Draw a picture or write about a bird nest you have seen.

Mom's Soup

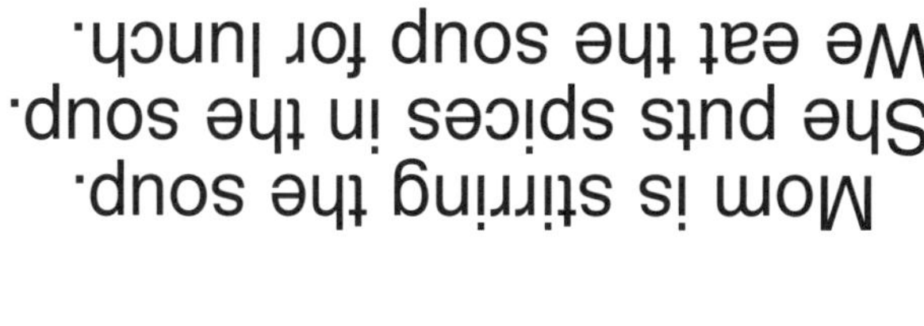

Mom is stirring the soup.
She puts spices in the soup.
We eat the soup for lunch.

Questions

1. Who is making soup?

____

____

2. What does she put in the soup?

____

____

3. When do they eat the soup?

____

____

- ❏ Talk about your favorite soup.
- ❏ Draw a picture or write about your favorite soup.

Cut on dotted line

Level 1

The Squirrel

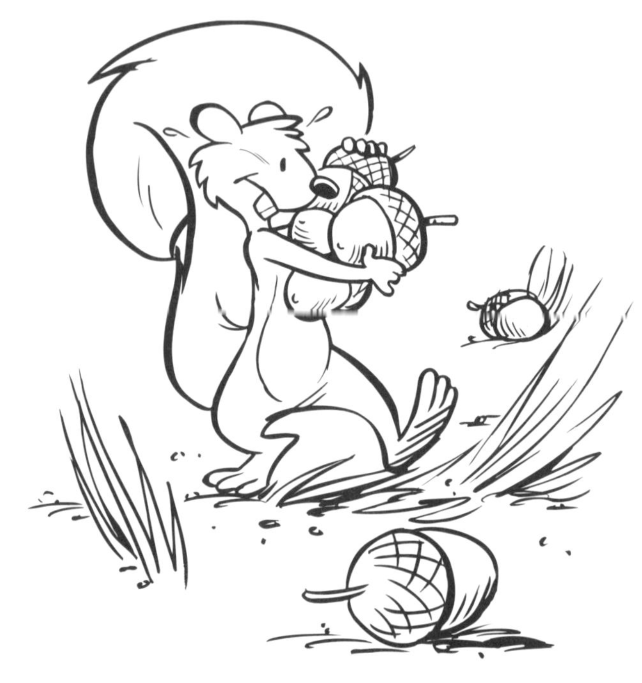

The gray squirrel picks up acorns from the ground. He hides them in a tree. In winter, he eats the acorns.

Questions

1. What color is the squirrel?

____

____

2. What does he hide in the tree?

____

____

3. When does he eat the acorns?

____

____

- ❏ Talk about a squirrel you have seen.
- ❏ Draw a picture or write about a squirrel you have seen.

Cut on dotted line

Brett's Plant

Brett fills the pot with dirt and seeds. He waters the seeds every day. The seeds grow into a green plant.

Questions

1. Who is this story about?

2. What does he do every day?

3. What do the seeds grow into?

❏ Talk about your favorite plant.

❏ Draw a picture or write about your favorite plant.

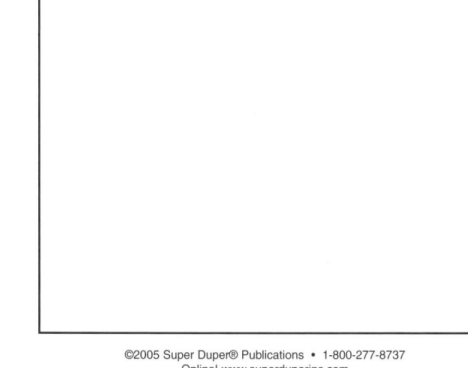

Jellybean John

John likes to eat jellybeans. Red and yellow jellybeans are his favorite. He eats jellybeans every day after school for a snack.

Questions

1. Who likes to eat jellybeans?

___

___

2. What color are his favorite jellybeans?

___

___

3. When does he eat jellybeans?

___

___

- ❏ Talk about your favorite snack.
- ❏ Draw a picture or write about your favorite snack.

Show and Tell

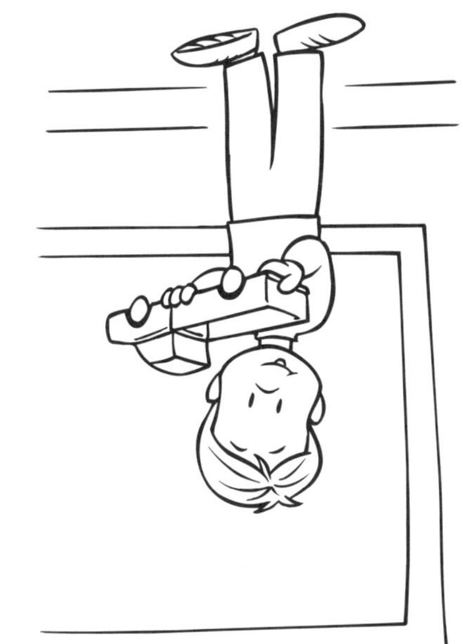

Today is show and tell at school. Zack shows his classmates his favorite truck. The truck is green.

Questions

1. What is today?

2. What does Zack show his classmates?

3. What color is the truck?

- ❑ Talk about your favorite toy.
- ❑ Draw a picture or write about your favorite toy.

Ice Cream Sundae

Dan puts a scoop of vanilla ice cream into a bowl. He puts whip cream and chocolate syrup on top. He eats it at the table.

Questions

1. What type of ice cream does Dan put in the bowl?

____

____

2. What does he put on top of the ice cream?

____

____

3. Where does he eat the sundae?

____

____

- ❏ Talk about your favorite ice cream sundae.
- ❏ Draw a picture or write about your favorite ice cream sundae.

Cut on dotted line

Loose Tooth

Kayla has a loose tooth. She wiggles the tooth and it comes out. She shows her mom the tooth.

Questions

1. Who has a loose tooth?

2. What happens when she wiggles the tooth?

3. Who does she show the tooth to?

- ❑ Talk about a time you had a loose tooth.
- ❑ Draw a picture or write about a time you had a loose tooth.

Spaghetti Again!

Grant sits down at the dinner table. Mom puts a plate of spaghetti in front of him. *"Great!"* he says, *"Spaghetti again!"*

Questions

1. Who sits down at the table?

____

____

2. What does his mom put in front of him?

____

____

3. What does he say?

____

____

- ❏ Talk about what you had last night for dinner.
- ❏ Draw a picture or write about what you had last night for dinner.

Cut on dotted line

Cut on dotted line

Level 1

Batter Up!

It's Corey's turn to bat. He picks up his bat and walks up to the plate. When he hits the ball, the crowd cheers.

Questions

1. Who is this story about?

2. What does he pick up?

3. What does the crowd do when he hits the ball?

- ❑ Talk about your favorite sport.
- ❑ Draw a picture or write about your favorite sport.

Andrew's Birthday

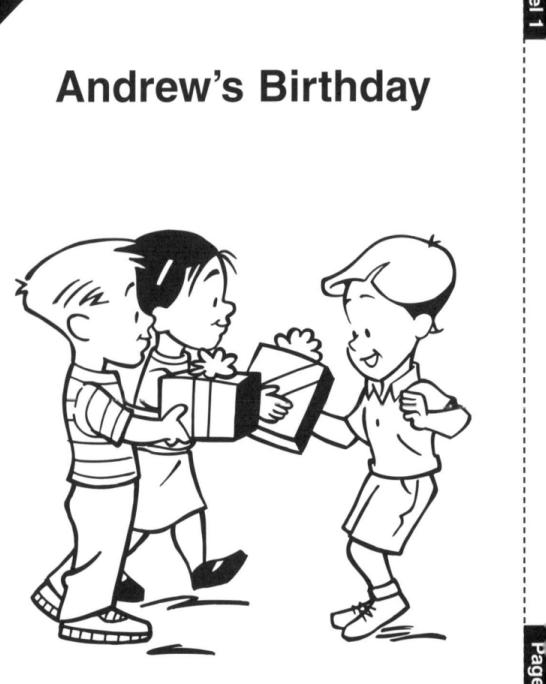

Today is Andrew's birthday. He invites his friends to his house for cake and ice cream. Each friend brings Andrew a birthday present.

Questions

1. Who is having a birthday?

2. What do Andrew and his friends eat?

3. What do Andrew's friends bring to the party?

- ❑ Talk about your last birthday.
- ❑ Draw a picture or write about your last birthday.

1 2 3 4

Cut on dotted line

Level 1

Tyler's Vacation

Tyler went camping with his mom and dad. Tyler and his dad caught a fish for dinner. They cooked the fish over the campfire.

Questions

1. Who went camping?

2. What did Tyler and his dad catch?

3. What did they do with the fish?

- ❑ Talk about what you would do on a camping trip.
- ❑ Draw a picture or write about what you would do on a camping trip.

Gym Class

Mitch likes gym class.
The gym teacher lets Mitch play soccer with his friends.
The gym teacher blows the whistle when class ends.

Questions

1. Who likes gym class?

2. What does he like to play?

3. What does the gym teacher do at the end of class?

- ❏ Talk about what you like to do in gym class.
- ❏ Draw a picture or write about what you like to do in gym class.

Ollie Owl

Ollie Owl sits high on a tree limb. He watches the deer as it eats. At night, he gathers his own food to eat.

Questions

1. Where is Ollie sitting?

2. Who does he watch eat?

3. What does he do at night?

- ❑ Talk about an owl you may have seen.
- ❑ Draw a picture or write about an owl you may have seen.

Fall Festival

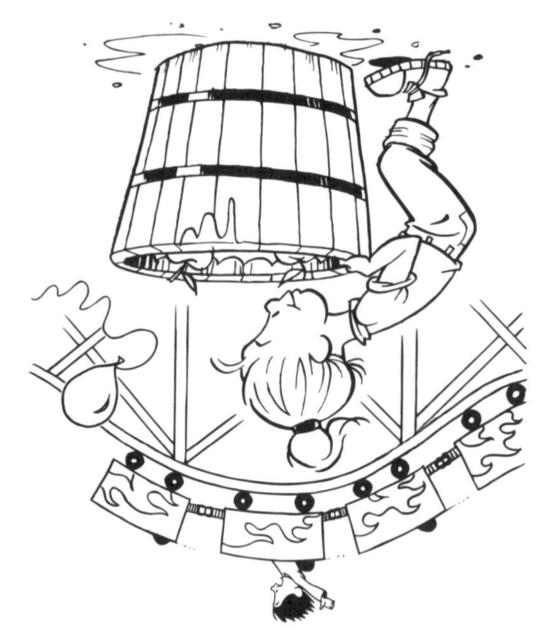

Madison and Todd go to the fall festival. Madison bobs for apples. Todd rides the new roller coaster.

Questions

1. Where do Madison and Todd go?

2. What does Madison do?

3. Who rides the new roller coaster?

- ❏ Talk about your favorite roller coaster.
- ❏ Draw a picture or write about your favorite roller coaster.

Cut on dotted line

Big Brother

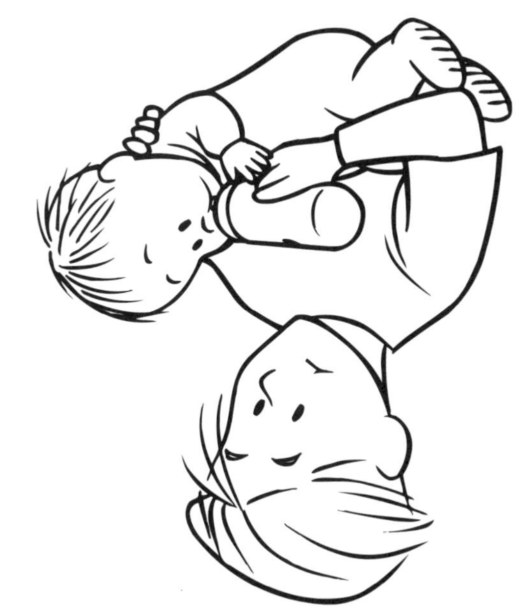

Dylan has a new baby brother named Kyle. Dylan feeds Kyle his bottle. Then, he puts Kyle in the crib.

Questions

1. Who has a new baby brother?

2. What is the baby's name?

3. Where does Dylan put Kyle?

- ❏ Talk about a time you have seen a new baby.
- ❏ Draw a picture or write about a time you have seen a new baby.

Let's Go to the Movies

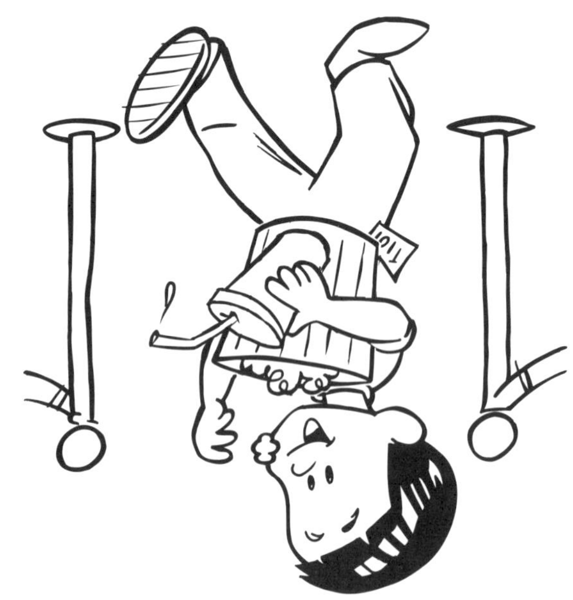

Lee buys a movie ticket. He gets popcorn and a drink. He sits in the front row to watch the movie.

Questions

1. Who is at the movies?

____

____

2. What does he buy to eat?

____

____

3. Where does he sit?

____

____

©2005 Super Duper® Publications

- ❑ Talk about a time you went to the movies.
- ❑ Draw a picture or write about a time you went to the movies.

The Park

José and Heather go to the park. They play on the swings and monkey bars. They buy hot dogs and chips.

Questions

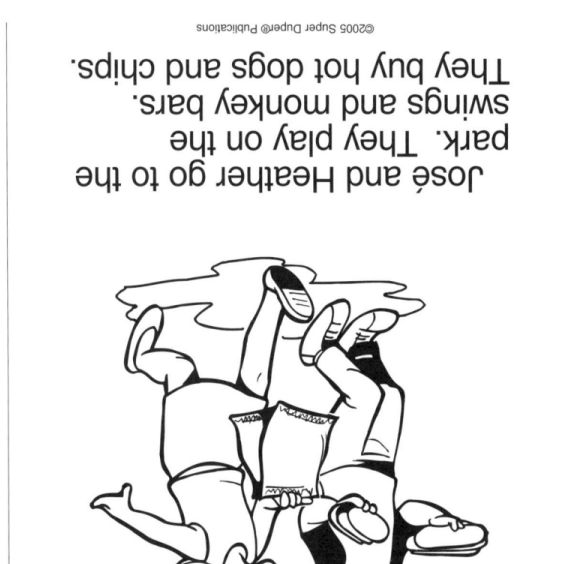

1. Who goes to the park?

2. What do they play on?

3. What do they eat?

- ❏ Talk about what you like to do at the park.
- ❏ Draw a picture or write about what you like to do at the park.

The Quarter

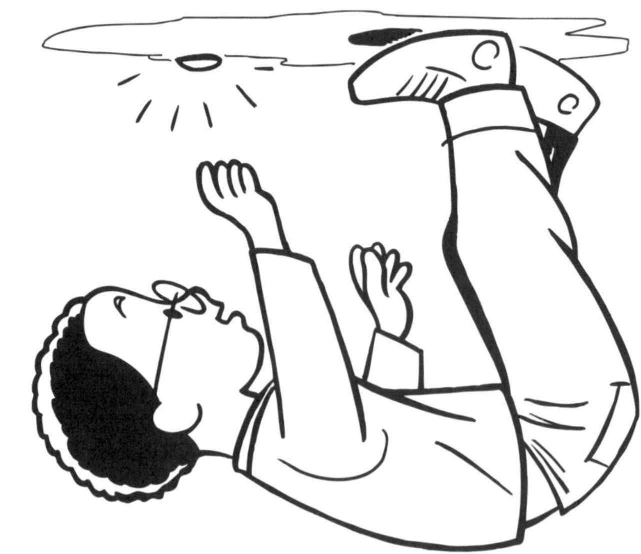

A shiny quarter is on the sidewalk. Mark picks up the quarter. He puts it in his piggy bank.

1 2 3 4

Questions

1. What is on the sidewalk?

2. Who picks up the quarter?

3. Where does he put the quarter?

- ❑ Talk about a time you found something outside.
- ❑ Draw a picture or write about a time you found something outside.

Jason's Dream

Jason has a dream about flying in the sky. He rides on a magic carpet. He sees all of his friends playing at the playground.

Questions

1. Who has a dream?

2. What does he ride on?

3. Who does he see?

- ❏ Talk about a time you had a dream.
- ❏ Draw a picture or write about a time you had a dream.

Scott's Valentine

Scott draws a Valentine card on red paper. He puts pink lace around the card. He puts the card on Amanda's desk.

Questions

1. Who draws a Valentine card?

2. What color lace does he put on the card?

3. Where does he put the card?

- ❏ Talk about a Valentine card you made.
- ❏ Draw a picture or write about a Valentine card you made.

Ski Day

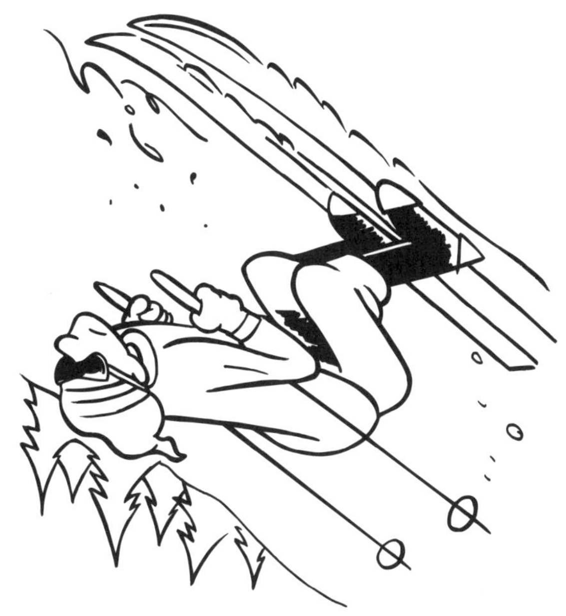

Nick buckles his new boots. He stands up and puts on his skis. He skis down the steep mountain.

Questions

1. Who is this story about?

2. What does he put on after his boots?

3. What does he ski down?

❏ Talk about what you like to do in winter.

❏ Draw a picture or write about what you like to do in winter.

©2005 Super Duper® Publications

Magic Trick

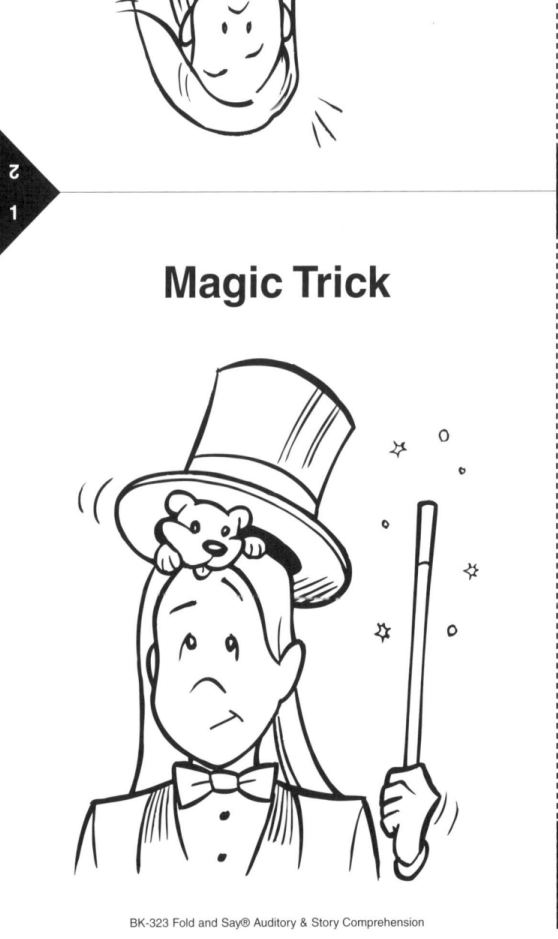

The magician puts a black hat on the table. She waves her wand over the hat. She reaches into the hat and pulls out a gopher!

Questions

1. What does the magician put on the table?

2. What does she wave over the hat?

3. What does she pull from the hat?

❑ Talk about your favorite magic trick.

❑ Draw a picture or write about your favorite magic trick.

Brenda's Cookies

Brenda is making cookies. The cookies have white icing on top. Brenda shares the cookies with her sister.

Questions

1. What is Brenda making?

___

2. What color is the icing?

___

3. Who does she share the cookies with?

___

- ❑ Talk about your favorite kind of cookie.
- ❑ Draw a picture or write about your favorite kind of cookie.

Cut on dotted line

Cut on dotted line

Level 1

Pam the Poodle

Pam the Poodle is clean. Her white fur is soft and shiny. Suddenly, she steps in a big puddle of mud!

Questions

1. Who is this story about?

2. What color is her fur?

3. What does she step in?

- ❑ Talk about a time you have gotten dirty.
- ❑ Draw a picture or write about a time you have gotten dirty.

Cut on dotted line

Level 1

Tina's Present

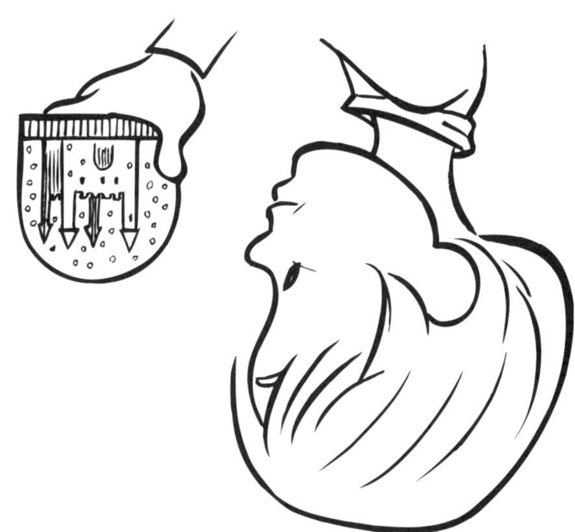

Tina gets a snow globe for her birthday. It has pink snowflakes in it. She shakes the globe and watches the snow fall.

Questions

1. What does Tina get for her birthday?

____

____

2. What color are the snowflakes?

____

____

3. What does she do with the globe?

____

____

- ❏ Talk about a present you received for your birthday.
- ❏ Draw a picture or write about a present you received for your birthday.

Cut on dotted line

Level 1

Joey Kangaroo

BK-323 Fold and Say® Auditory & Story Comprehension

Cathy Kangaroo hops to Zany Zebra's house. Cathy shows Zany her baby kangaroo named Joey. Joey is sleeping in Cathy's pouch.

Questions

1. Where is Cathy Kangaroo going?

2. What is her baby's name?

3. What is Joey doing?

- ❏ Talk about your favorite animal.
- ❏ Draw a picture or write about your favorite animal.

The Band

Ian is in the school band. He plays the drums. He plays during halftime at the football games.

Questions

1. Who is in the band?

2. What does he play?

3. When does he play at the football games?

- ❏ Talk about your favorite musical instrument.
- ❏ Draw a picture or write about your favorite musical instrument.

Cheese Time

Marty Mouse peeks out his mouse hole. He sees cheese on the counter. He gets the cheese and takes it back to his mouse hole.

Questions

1. Who is this story about?

2. What does he see on the counter?

3. Where does he take the cheese?

- ❏ Talk about your favorite food.
- ❏ Draw a picture or write about your favorite food.

1 2 3 4

Tara is excited. Today, her grandparents are coming to visit. They will stay with her family for one week.

Questions

1. Who is excited?

___

___

2. When are her grandparents coming to visit?

___

___

3. How long will they stay?

___

___

2 3
1 4

Visit with the Grandparents

- ❏ Talk about a time you visited your relatives.
- ❏ Draw a picture or write about a time you visited your relatives.

The Rodeo

Adam goes to the rodeo. He sees cowboys. He wears his cowboy hat and boots.

Questions

1. Where does Adam go?

2. What does he see?

3. What does he wear?

©2005 Super Duper® Publications

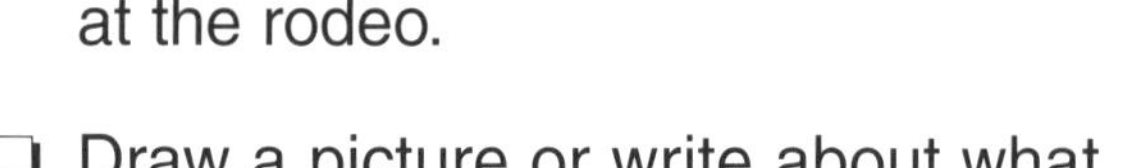

- ❏ Talk about what you would like to see at the rodeo.
- ❏ Draw a picture or write about what you would like to see at the rodeo.

Fireworks

Tonight is the fireworks show. Lynn invites her friend, Amy, over to watch. They see the fireworks from the backyard.

Questions

1. When is the fireworks show?

____

____

2. Who does Lynn invite to watch the fireworks?

____

____

3. Where do they watch the fireworks?

____

____

❏ Talk about a time you saw fireworks.

❏ Draw a picture or write about a time you saw fireworks.

Tea Party

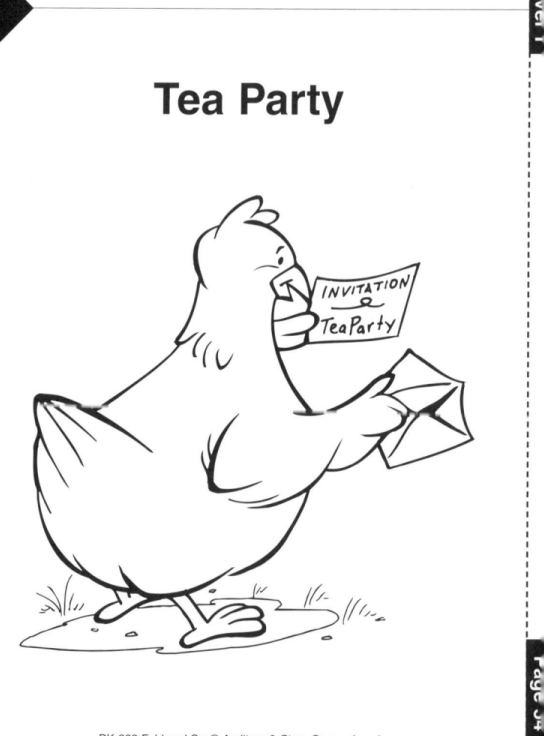

Rita Raccoon invites her friends over for a tea party. The party will be on Saturday. Rita will make a chocolate cake.

Questions

1. Who is having a tea party?

2. When is the tea party?

3. What does Rita make for the tea party?

- ❏ Talk about what happens at a tea party.
- ❏ Draw a picture or write about what happens at a tea party.

Chris the Clown

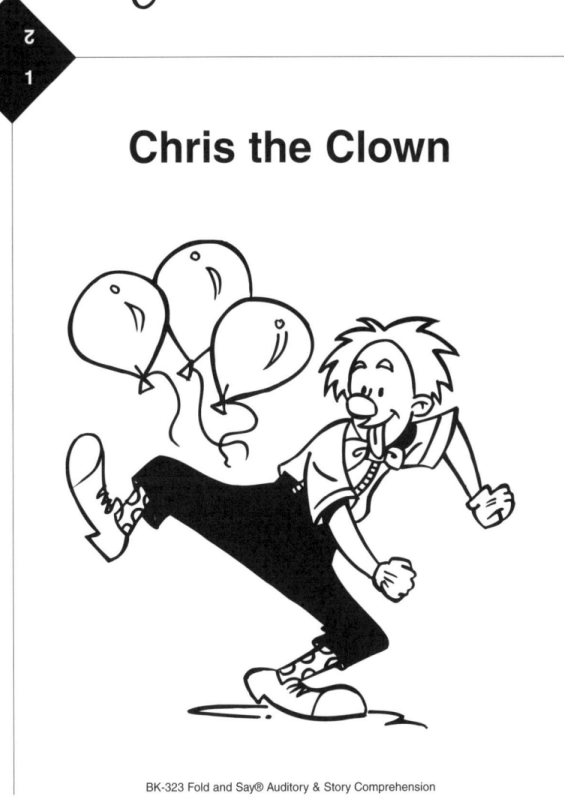

Chris the Clown wears big shoes. He has a red nose and orange hair. He likes to make children laugh.

Questions

1. Who wears big shoes?

2. What color is his hair?

3. Who does he like to make laugh?

- ❑ Talk about a time you have seen a clown.
- ❑ Draw a picture or write about a time you have seen a clown.

The Soccer Game

Dad and Jeremy are at a soccer game. They sit on the sidelines. They clap and cheer for their team to win.

Questions

1. Who is at the soccer game?

____

____

2. Where do they sit?

____

____

3. Who do they clap and cheer for?

____

____

- ❑ Talk about a time you watched a sports game.
- ❑ Draw a picture or write about a time you watched a sports game.

The Butterfly

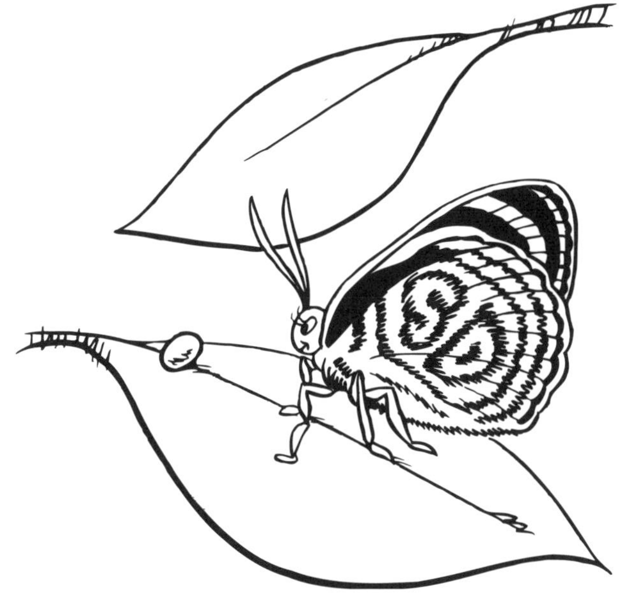

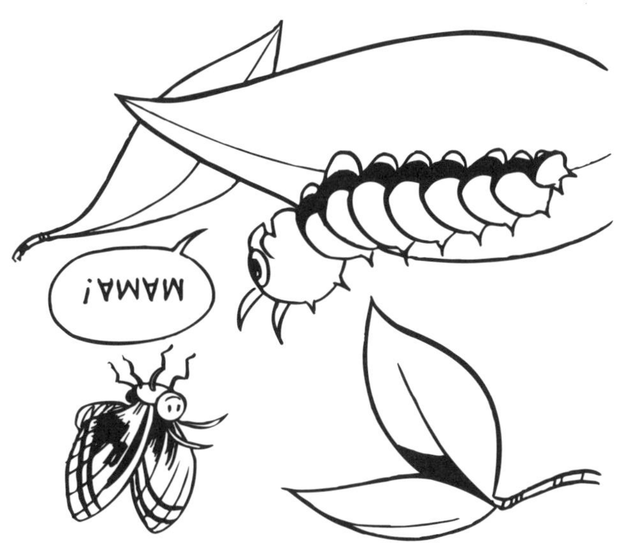

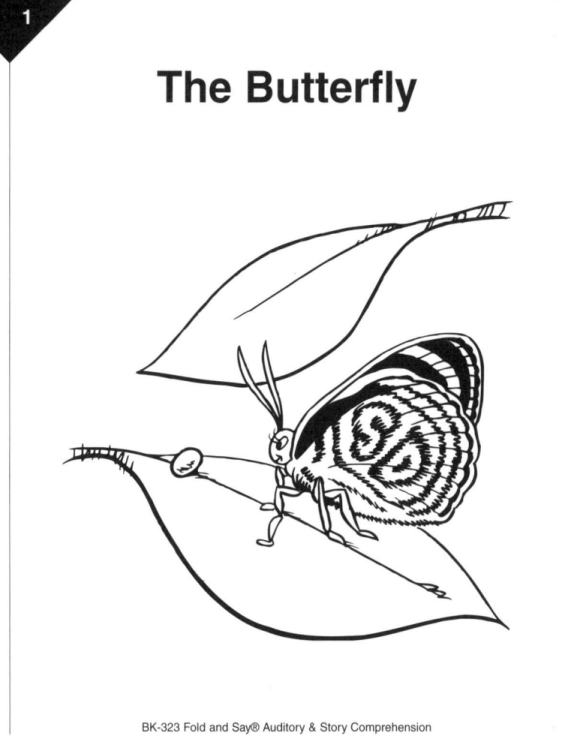

The butterfly lays an egg on a tree leaf. The egg turns into a black caterpillar. Later, the caterpillar becomes a beautiful butterfly.

Questions

1. Where does the butterfly lay the egg?

____

____

2. What color caterpillar does the egg turn into?

____

____

3. What does the caterpillar become?

____

____

❏ Talk about a time you have seen a butterfly.

❏ Draw a picture or write about a time you have seen a butterfly.

Golf

Todd is learning to play golf. He takes golf lessons on Tuesday afternoons. He has a new black golf bag.

Questions

1. Who is learning to play golf?

2. When are his golf lessons?

3. What color is his new golf bag?

- ❏ Talk about a game or sport you would like to play.
- ❏ Draw a picture or write about a game or sport you would like to play.

A Fast Cat

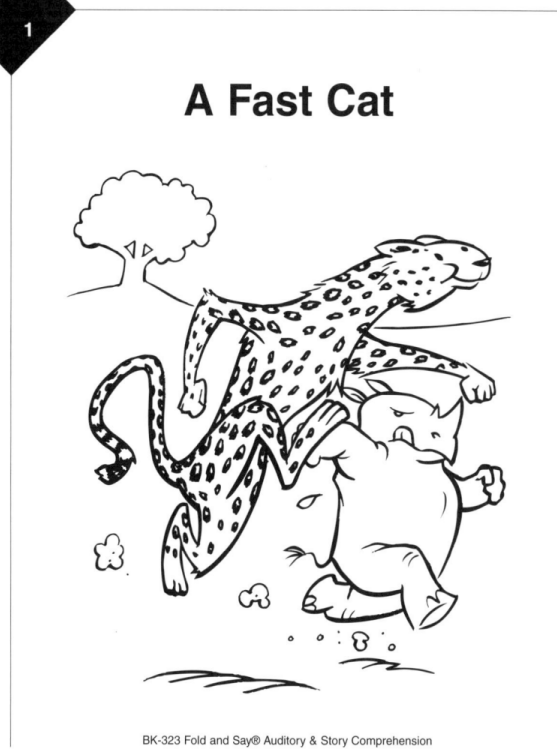

Chase the Cheetah is a fast cat. He runs faster than cars and trains. He likes to race his friends in the jungle.

Questions

1. Who is a fast cat?

____

____

2. What can he run faster than?

____

____

3. Who does he like to race?

____

____

- ❏ Talk about your favorite wild animal.
- ❏ Draw a picture or write about your favorite wild animal.

New Teacher

Lindsay has a new second grade teacher. Her name is Mrs. Wilson. Every day, Mrs. Wilson wears a purple sweater to school.

Questions

1. Who has a new teacher?

____

____

2. What is the new teacher's name?

____

____

3. What does she wear every day?

____

____

- ❏ Talk about a time you have had a new teacher.
- ❏ Draw a picture or write about a time you have had a new teacher.

Snow Day

BK-323 Fold and Say® Auditory & Story Comprehension

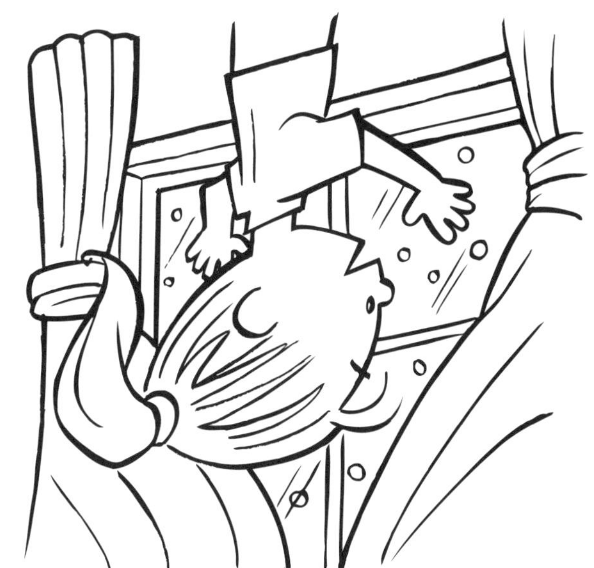
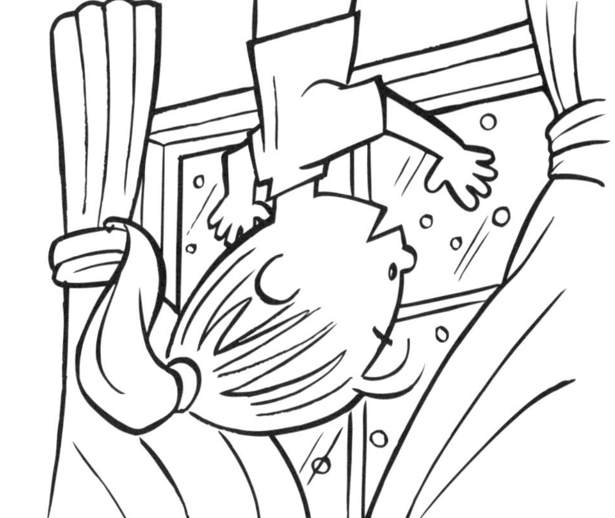

Sara looks out the window.
Snow is falling from the sky.
The snow covers the mailbox and trees.

Questions

1. Who looks out the window?

____

____

2. What is falling from the sky?

____

____

3. What does the snow cover?

____

____

- ❑ Talk about a time you have seen snow.
- ❑ Draw a picture or write about a time you have seen snow.

Pizza Friday

Michael likes Friday lunch at school. Friday is always pizza day. He likes his pizza with extra cheese.

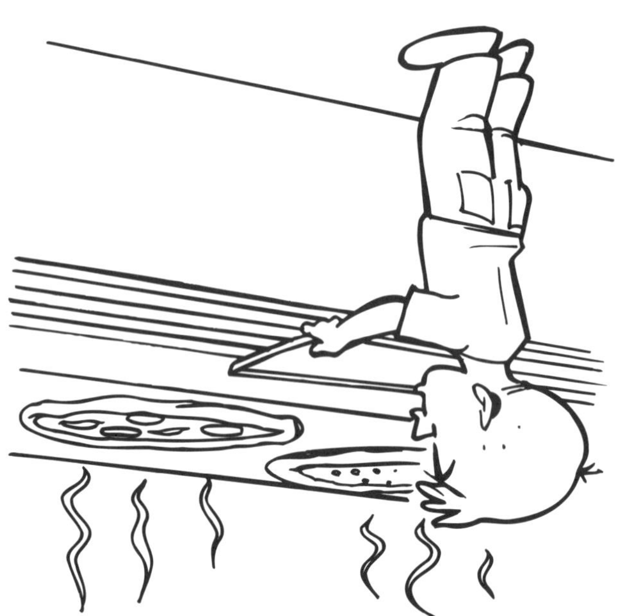

Questions

1. Who is this story about?

2. What is for lunch on Friday?

3. What does he like on his pizza?

- ❏ Talk about your favorite lunch at school.
- ❏ Draw a picture or write about your favorite lunch at school.

Cut on dotted line

Level 1

Level 2 Stories

Buried Treasure

Andy and Jamie like to play pirates at the beach. They dig a hole near the water. *"I feel something,"* says Andy. They look in the hole and see a shiny seashell. Jamie picks up the seashell and puts it to his ear.

What is the main idea of this story?

a. Shovels dig holes.
b. All seashells are shiny.
c. Andy and Jamie find a seashell.

Questions

1. What do Andy and Jamie like to play?

2. Where do they play?

3. What do they find in the hole?

❑ Talk about what you would like to find if you were digging for buried treasure.

❑ Draw a picture or write about what you would like to find if you were digging for buried treasure.

Cut on dotted line

Brian the Bullfrog

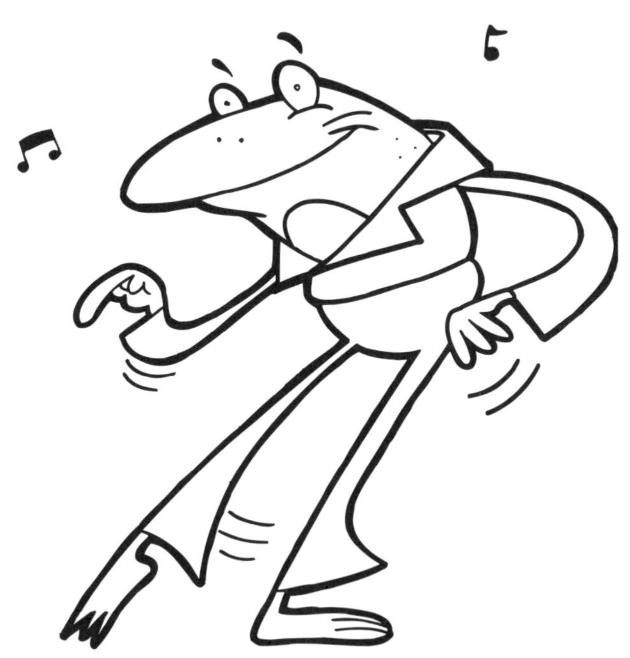

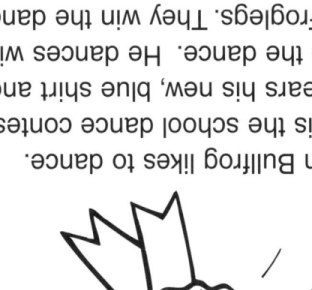

Brian Bullfrog likes to dance. Tonight is the school dance contest. Brian wears his new, blue shirt and pants to the dance. He dances with Freida Frogleqs. They win the dance contest!

What is the main idea of this story?

a. Frogs can dance.

b. Freida is a better dancer.

c. Brian and Freida are in a dance contest.

Questions

1. What does Brian Bullfrog like to do?

____

____

2. What is tonight?

____

____

3. What do Brian and Freida win?

____

____

- ❑ Talk about a time you were in a contest.
- ❑ Draw a picture or write about a time you were in a contest.

Best Friends

Cut on dotted line

Tina and Nora are best friends. They like to do things together. On Saturdays, they have a picnic at the lake. They eat sandwiches, and cake for dessert. Afterwards, they go swimming in the lake.

What is the main idea of this story?

a. Only girls can swim.
b. Tina and Nora go to the lake.
c. Everyone should eat sandwiches.

Questions

1. Who are best friends?

____

____

2. Where do they go on Saturdays?

____

____

3. What do they eat?

____

____

1 2 3 4

- ❏ Talk about what you like to do with your friends.
- ❏ Draw a picture or write about what you like to do with your friends.

Danny Dragon

Danny Dragon lives in a castle. He likes to eat dessert. For breakfast, he eats vanilla ice cream. At lunch, the castle cook makes Danny cupcakes. He has a stomachache from eating so many desserts.

What is the main idea of this story?

a. Danny likes to eat vegetables.

b. Danny lives in the forest.

c. Danny eats desserts.

Questions

1. Where does Danny Dragon live?

____

____

2. What does he eat for breakfast?

____

____

3. When does he eat cupcakes?

____

____

- ❑ Talk about your favorite dessert.
- ❑ Draw a picture or write about your favorite dessert.

Mom's Birthday

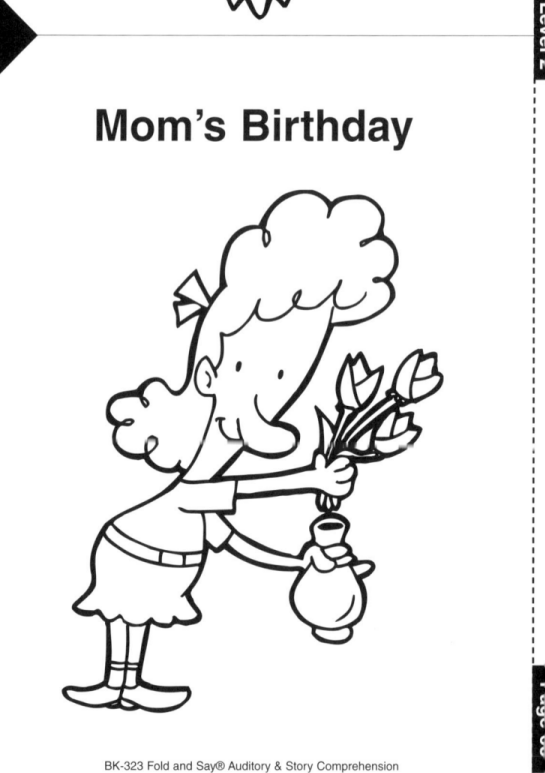

Today is Mom's birthday. Molly wants to do something special for her. Molly picks red and yellow tulips from the garden. She puts the flowers in a vase for Mom.

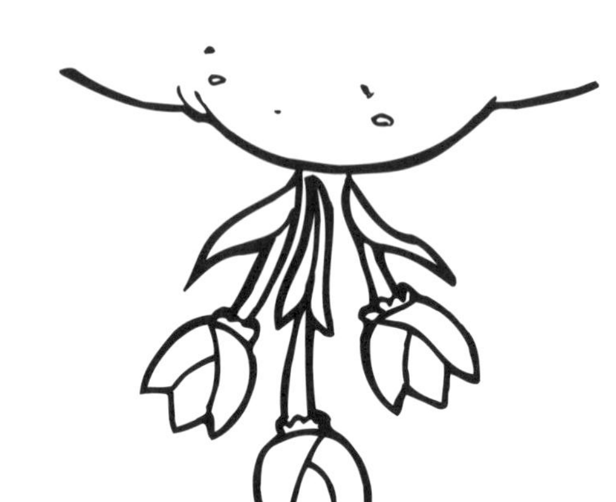

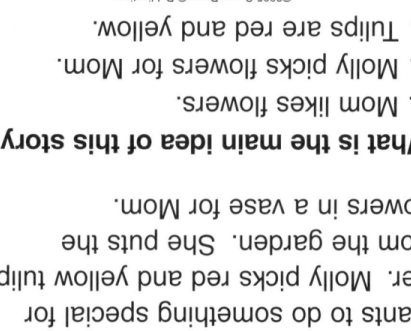

What is the main idea of this story?

a. Mom likes flowers.
b. Molly picks flowers for Mom.
c. Tulips are red and yellow.

Questions

1. When is Mom's birthday?

____

____

2. What color tulips does Molly pick?

____

____

3. What does she put the flowers in?

____

____

❏ Talk about how you celebrate your parent or caregiver's birthday.

❏ Draw a picture or write about how you celebrate your parent or caregiver's birthday.

The Tallest Animal

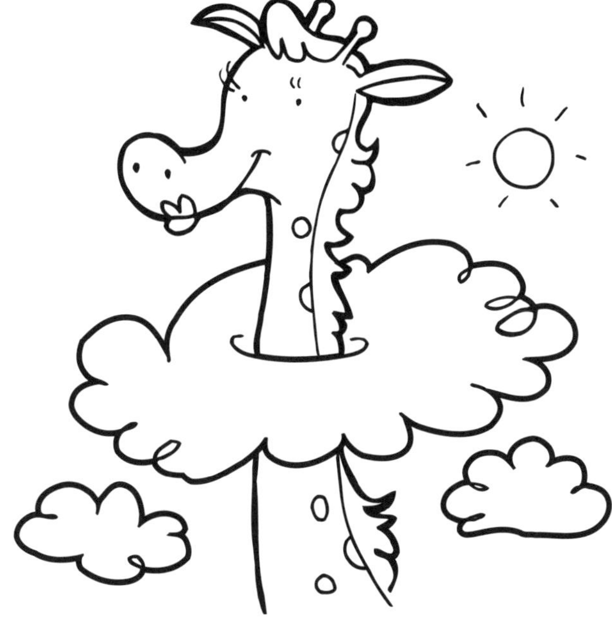

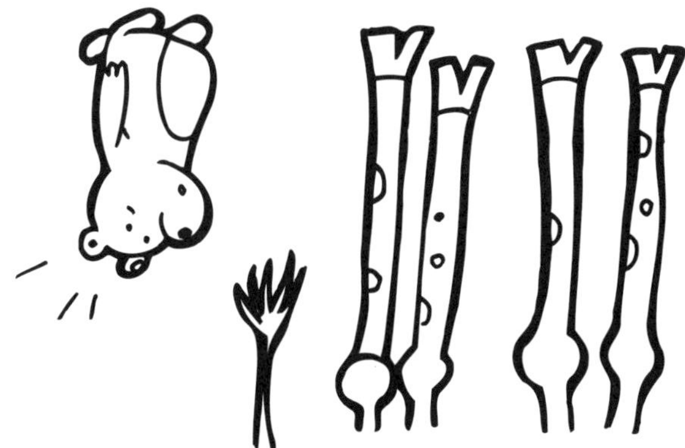

Ginny Giraffe is the tallest animal in the jungle. She is so tall she can see above the trees. Her neck and legs are long. Sometimes, it seems her head is touching the clouds.

What is the main idea of this story?

a. Ginny is tall.

b. All giraffes heads touch the clouds.

c. Ginny lives in the jungle.

Questions

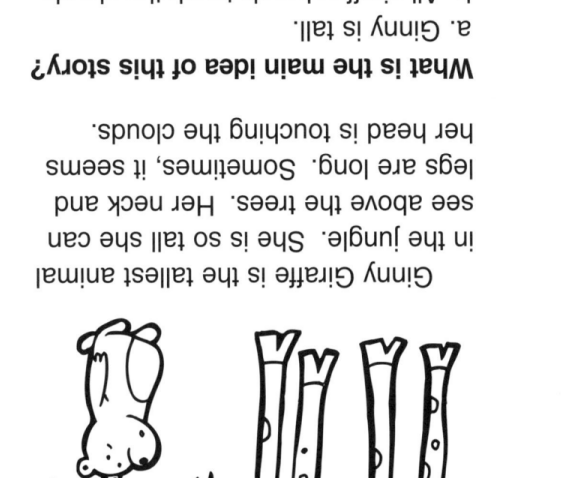

1. Who is this story about?

___

___

2. Where does Ginny live?

___

___

3. Which of Ginny's body parts are long?

___

___

- ❑ Talk about your favorite animal.
- ❑ Draw a picture or write about your favorite animal.

Calling 911

Steve smelled smoke. He looked across the street and saw his neighbor's house on fire. Steve ran to the phone and dialed 911. He told the operator the address of the fire.

What is the main idea of this story?

a. Steve can use a phone.

b. Steve saw a house on fire and called 911.

c. Steve plays outside across the street.

Questions

1. Who smelled smoke?

____

____

2. Whose house was on fire?

____

____

3. What did he tell the operator?

____

____

- ❑ Talk about what you would do in case of an emergency.
- ❑ Draw a picture or write about what you would do in case of an emergency.

The Ballerina

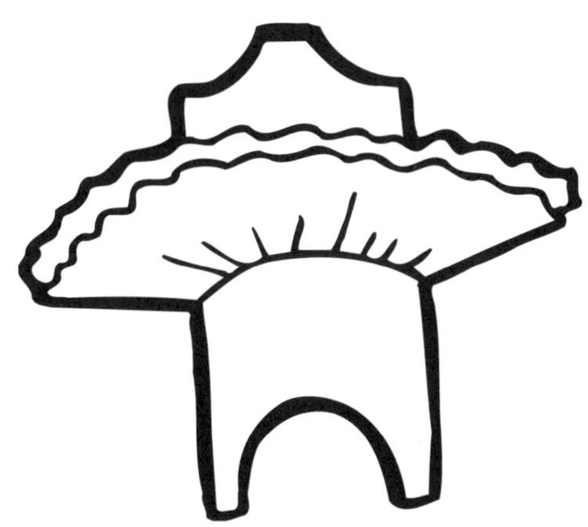

Ingrid wants to be a ballerina when she gets older. Today is ballet class. She wears a pink leotard and black slippers. The music begins and Ingrid starts to dance.

What is the main idea of this story?

a. Ingrid likes pink.
b. Ingrid is at ballet class.
c. Today Ingrid wears slippers.

Questions

1. Who wants to be a ballerina?

____

____

2. What is today?

____

____

3. What does she wear to class?

____

____

- ❑ Talk about what you want to be when you get older.
- ❑ Draw a picture or write about what you want to be when you get older.

Lucy Ladybug

Lucy Ladybug lives under a tree leaf. She likes to play with her friend, Beth Bee. Lucy and Beth like to fly around Mrs. Rabbit's garden. They eat tomatoes from the garden.

What is the main idea of this story?

a. Beth is a bee.
b. Lucy lives under a tree leaf.
c. Lucy and Beth are friends.

Questions

1. Where does Lucy Ladybug live?

____

____

2. Who does she like to play with?

____

____

3. What do they eat in the garden?

____

____

- ❏ Talk about what you like to do with your friends.
- ❏ Draw a picture or write about what you like to do with your friends.

Cool Dad

My dad is cool. He rides a shiny, black motorcycle and takes me places. He wears a red bandana around his neck. We both wear matching bright, yellow helmets.

What is the main idea of this story?

a. My dad rides a motorcycle.
b. Motorcycles are black.
c. Only dads can wear bandanas.

Questions

1. What does Dad ride?

2. What does Dad wear around his neck?

3. What color are the helmets?

- ❑ Talk about a time you went somewhere with a parent or caregiver.
- ❑ Draw a picture or write about a time you went somewhere with a parent or caregiver.

Soccer Star

Amanda plays soccer. She is very talented and always gets to start the game. Amanda makes more goals than any other player. Her coach even gave her the "star" player award.

What is the main idea of this story?

a. Amanda is a good soccer player.

b. Amanda likes her coach.

c. Amanda got an award.

Questions

1. What does Amanda play?

____

____

2. What does Amanda make more of than any other player?

____

____

3. Who gave Amanda the award?

____

____

- ❑ Talk about something you are good at.
- ❑ Draw a picture or write about something you are good at.

The Big Game

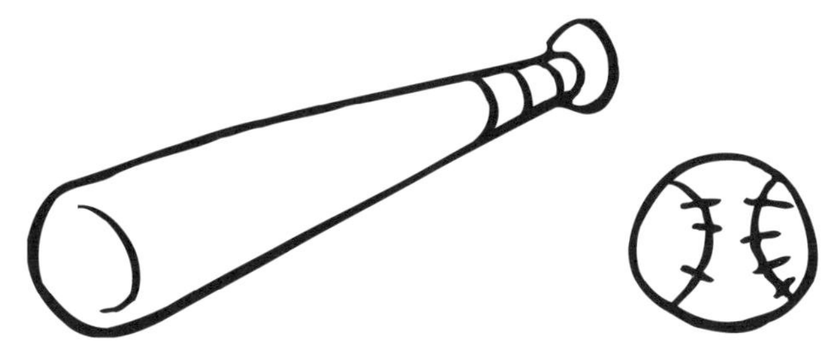

Today is the championship softball game. Lindsey and her teammates listen to the coach give instructions. Lindsey is the pitcher. She puts on her purple jersey and runs out to the pitcher's mound.

What is the main idea of this story?

a. Lindsey wears a jersey.

b. Lindsey listens to the coach.

c. Lindsey plays softball.

1 2 3 4

Questions

1. What is today?

____

____

2. Who is the pitcher?

____

____

3. What color jersey does she wear?

____

____

- ❏ Talk about what you think happens next.
- ❏ Draw a picture or write about what you think happens next.

Leo's Pet

Leo has a pet lizard named Lizzy. Lizzy is green with white spots. Lizzy lives in a glass cage. Leo feeds Lizzy bugs and insects.

What is the main idea of this story?

a. Lizards are only green.

b. Lizards make good pets.

c. Lizzy is a pet lizard.

Questions

1. Who has a pet lizard?

2. What color is Lizzy?

3. What does Leo feed her?

- ❑ Talk about the kind of pet you would like to have.
- ❑ Draw a picture or write about the kind of pet you would like to have.

Tractor Rides

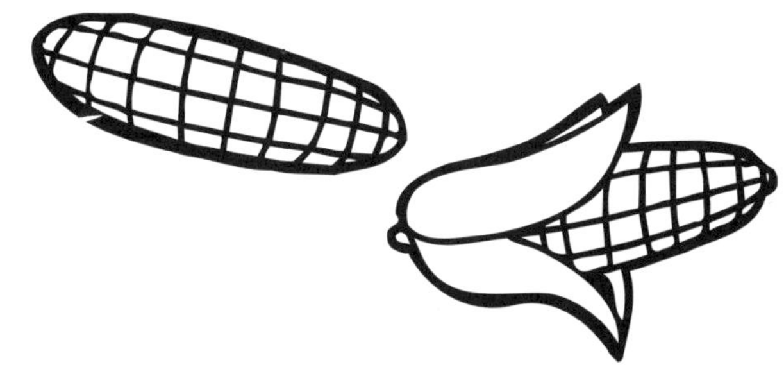

Kay likes to go for tractor rides with Grandpa. They ride around the vegetable fields. Sometimes, Grandpa lets Kay steer the tractor. She steers the tractor up and down the rows of corn.

What is the main idea of this story?

a. Grandpa drives a tractor.
b. Kay and Grandpa drive the tractor.
c. Kay likes the vegetable fields.

Questions

1. What does Kay like to do?

____

____

2. Where do they ride the tractor?

____

____

3. What does Grandpa let Kay do?

____

____

- ❑ Talk about what you like to do with your grandparent(s).
- ❑ Draw a picture or write about what you like to do with your grandparent(s).

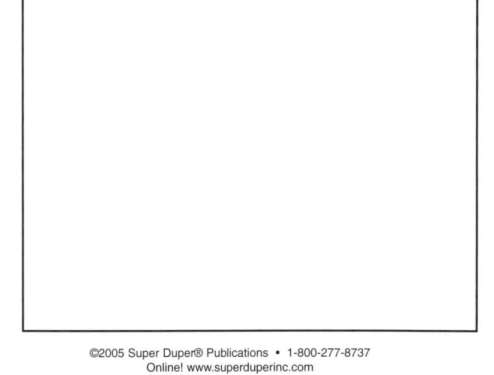

Lost Pet

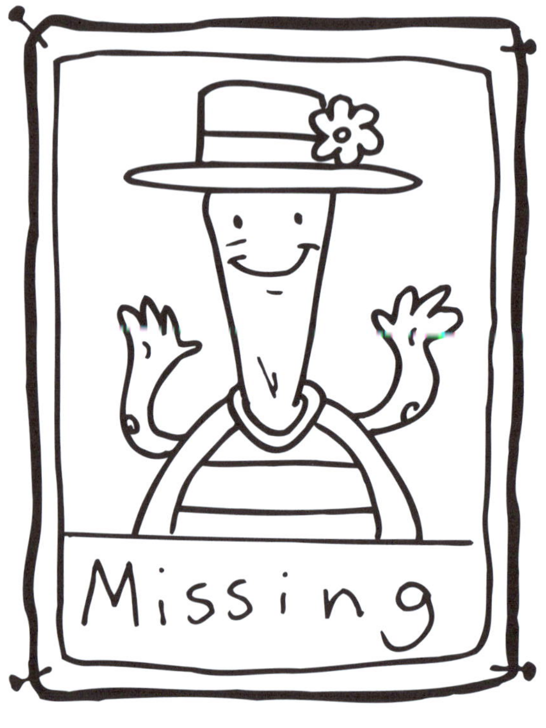

Mike is sad because his pet turtle is missing. He looks all over his room for the turtle. Finally, he finds the turtle hiding in the closet. Mike feels much better now!

What is the main idea of this story?

a. Mike lost his pet turtle.
b. Mike is sad.
c. Turtles like to hide.

Questions

1. Who is sad?

____

2. What is missing?

____

3. Where does he find the turtle?

____

❏ Talk about a time you lost something.
❏ Draw a picture or write about a time you lost something.

The Artist

Jake likes to paint pictures of animals. He paints a picture of his bird, Squeaky. He paints Squeaky red. He puts the picture in his room on the wall near his bed.

What is the main idea of this story?

a. Squeaky is red.
b. Only boys can paint.
c. Jake paints a picture of Squeaky.

Questions

1. Who likes to paint?

____

____

2. What does he paint?

____

____

3. Where does he put the painting?

____

____

- ❑ Talk about your favorite hobby.
- ❑ Draw a picture or write about your favorite hobby.

The Magic Carpet

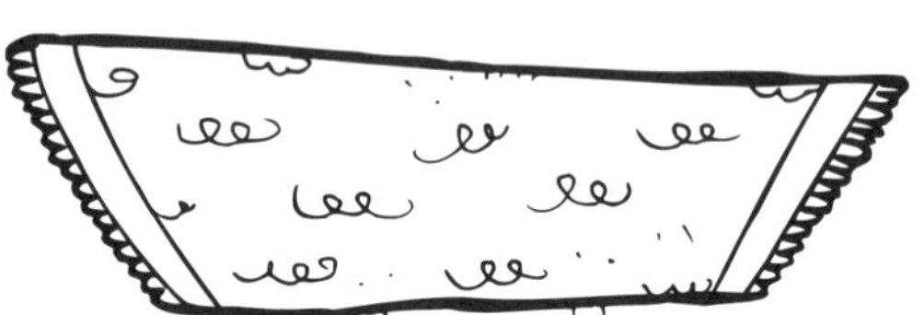

Keisha finds an old carpet in the basement. She unfolds it and puts it on the floor. Suddenly, the carpet rises off the ground! Keisha jumps on the carpet and rides it around the house.

What is the main idea of this story?

a. Carpets can fly.
b. Keisha takes a ride on a carpet.
c. Carpets are kept in the basement.

Questions

1. Who is this story about?

____

2. What does she find in the basement?

____

3. Where does she ride the carpet?

____

- ❏ Talk about a time you found something old.
- ❏ Draw a picture or write about a time you found something old.

Greg's Party

Greg is excited. Today is his birthday party. Mom makes a chocolate birthday cake. His friends sing "Happy Birthday." After everyone eats some cake, Greg opens his gifts.

What is the main idea of this story?

a. Greg is having a birthday party.
b. Greg likes presents.
c. Mom makes a cake.

Questions

1. Who is having a birthday party?

2. What does Mom make?

3. What do his friends sing?

- ❑ Talk about your favorite birthday.
- ❑ Draw a picture or write about your favorite birthday.

Cut on dotted line

Level 2

The Dude Ranch

Joe's family visits a dude ranch for vacation. There are many fun things to do on a dude ranch. Joe learns how to lasso a pony. On the last night, he goes on a hayride.

What is the main idea of this story?

a. Ponies live on dude ranches.
b. Joe's family is at a dude ranch.
c. Joe learns to lasso a pony.

Questions

1. Where does Joe's family go on vacation?

___

___

2. What does Joe learn to do on vacation?

___

___

3. What does he do on the last night?

___

___

- ❑ Talk about what you did on your last family vacation.
- ❑ Draw a picture or write about what you did on your last family vacation.

Drive with Dad

Dad and Michelle take a drive in the mountains. It's a warm, sunny day. They ride in Dad's new, red truck. Michelle looks out the window and sees many pine trees.

What is the main idea of this story?

a. Trees grow in the mountains.
b. Trucks are red.
c. Dad and Michelle drive in the mountains.

Questions

1. Who is driving in the mountains?

2. What color truck does Dad drive?

3. What does Michelle see out the window?

- ❑ Talk about what you like to see in the mountains.
- ❑ Draw a picture or write about you like to see in the mountains.

Sleepy Alex

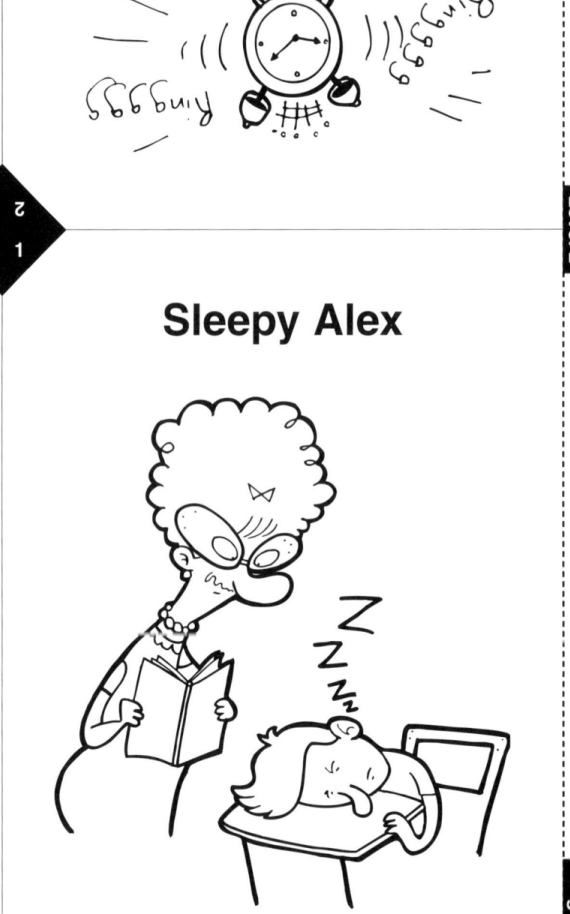

Alex went to bed late last night. He woke up late for school. He was so sleepy that he yawned all day long. He even fell asleep during math class.

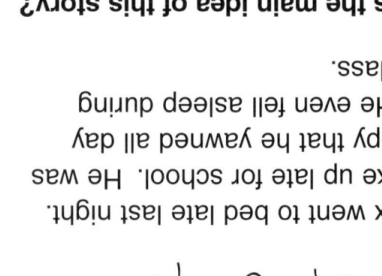

What is the main idea of this story?

a. Alex was sleepy.
b. Alex rode the bus to school.
c. Yawning is a bad habit.

Questions

1. Who is sleepy?

____

____

2. What did he do all day?

____

____

3. What did he do during math class?

____

____

- ❏ Talk about a time you were sleepy.
- ❏ Draw a picture or write about a time you were sleepy.

Cut on dotted line

Beach Fun

Carol is wearing her pink swimsuit to the beach. She puts her goggles over her eyes. She grabs her boogie board and runs into the ocean. She rides the boogie board on the waves.

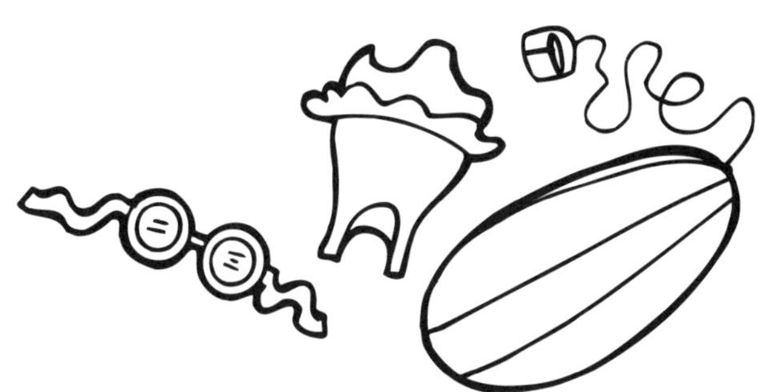

What is the main idea of this story?

a. Carol has a new pair of goggles.

b. Carol knows how to swim.

c. Carol plays at the beach.

Questions

1. What color is Carol's swimsuit?

2. What does Carol put over her eyes?

3. What does she ride in the water?

- ❏ Talk about what you like to do at the beach.
- ❏ Draw a picture or write about what you like to do at the beach.

Stella's Web

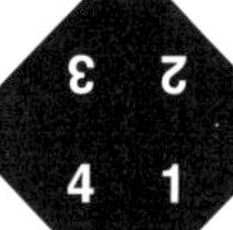

Stella Spider is busy spinning a web for her home. She makes a big beautiful web. The web is very sticky. Stella loves her new home in the corner of the room.

What is the main idea of this story?

a. Spiders are busy.
b. Stella Spider is making her home.
c. The web is sticky.

Questions

1. What is Stella making?

____

____

2. How does the web feel?

____

____

3. Where is the web?

____

____

©2005 Super Duper® Publications

- ❑ Talk about a spider web you have seen.
- ❑ Draw a picture or write about a spider web you have seen.

Super Detective

BK-323 Fold and Say® Auditory & Story Comprehension

Mom lost her favorite pair of shoes. Max searched for the shoes. He looked all over the house. He found the shoes in the garage.

What is the main idea of this story?

a. Only boys can find lost shoes.
b. Mom wears shoes.
c. Max looked for Mom's pair of shoes.

Questions

1. What did Mom lose?

____

____

2. Who looked for them?

____

____

3. Where did he find them?

____

____

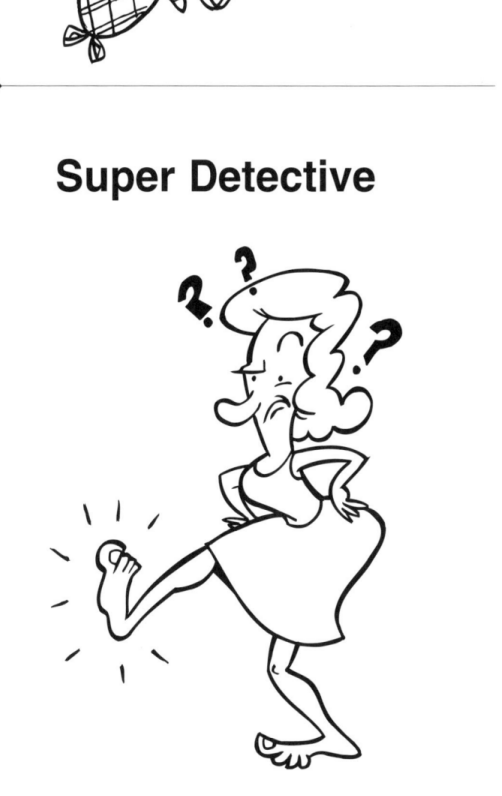

- ❏ Talk about a time you found something for your parent or caregiver.
- ❏ Draw a picture or write about a time you found something for your parent or caregiver.

The Pumpkin

Jill picks a large, orange pumpkin from the pumpkin patch. Dad and Jill carve the pumpkin. They carve a silly face on it. They put the pumpkin on the front porch.

What is the main idea of this story?

a. Jill likes pumpkins.

b. Pumpkins are large.

c. Dad and Jill carve the pumpkin.

Questions

1. Who goes to the pumpkin patch?

2. Who helps her carve the pumpkin?

3. Where do they put the pumpkin?

1 2 3 4

- ❏ Talk about a pumpkin you carved.
- ❏ Draw a picture or write about a pumpkin you carved.

Melanie's Cookies

Melanie gets out butter, milk, and flour. She mixes the ingredients in the bowl. She puts the batter in the oven. Soon the batter bakes into tasty cookies.

What is the main idea of this story?

a. Melanie is making cookies.
b. Melanie can cook.
c. Cookies need to bake in the oven.

Questions

1. Who is this story about?

2. What does she mix together?

3. What does the batter turn into?

- ❑ Talk about your favorite type of cookie.
- ❑ Draw a picture or write about your favorite type of cookie.

Birthday Present

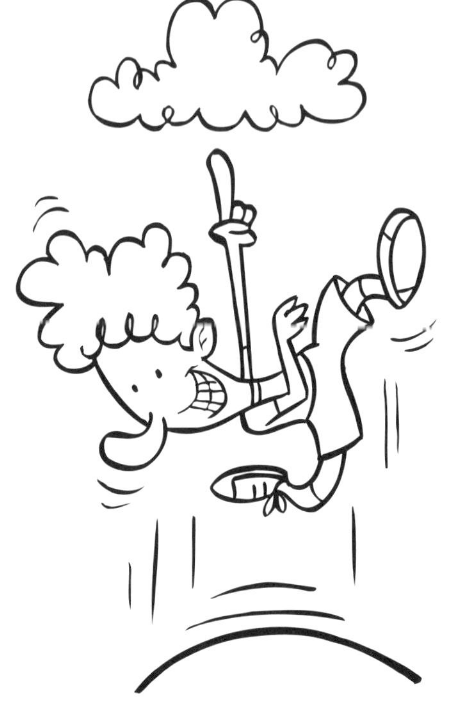

Today is Todd's birthday. His parents give him a trampoline for his birthday. Todd jumps on the trampoline all afternoon. He jumps so high, he can almost touch the sky!

What is the main idea of this story?

a. Trampolines are fun.
b. Todd gets a trampoline.
c. Only boys can jump on trampolines.

Questions

1. Whose birthday is today?

2. What does he get for his birthday?

3. What can he almost touch?

©2005 Super Duper® Publications

- ❑ Talk about a present you received for your birthday.
- ❑ Draw a picture or write about a present you received for your birthday.

Koala Bears

Koala bears live in trees in Australia. They use their sharp claws to hold onto the trees. They live in trees to protect themselves from other animals. They like to eat eucalyptus tree leaves.

What is the main idea of this story?

a. Koala bears are small.
b. Koala bears have sharp claws.
c. Koala bears live in trees.

Questions

1. Where do koala bears live?

____

____

2. What do they use to hold onto trees?

____

____

3. What do they eat?

____

____

- ❏ Talk about an animal you think is interesting.
- ❏ Draw a picture or write about an animal you think is interesting.

Message in a Bottle

Brent walks down the beach. He sees a bottle with a cork in it, lying in the sand. He opens the bottle and finds a message. It says, *"Please be my pen pal and write to me."*

What is the main idea of this story?

a. Brent finds a bottle on the beach.
b. Brent likes the beach.
c. Bottles have messages inside.

Questions

1. Who is walking on the beach?

2. What does he find in the sand?

3. What does the message say?

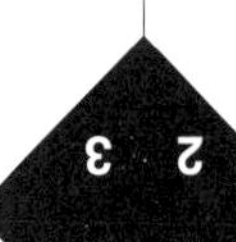

- ❏ Talk about what you think might happen next.
- ❏ Draw a picture or write about what you think might happen next.

Class News Reporter

Jason is the class news reporter. He writes stories about what is happening at school. He puts his stories in the school newspaper. His classmates like reading his stories.

What is the main idea of this story?

a. Jason goes to school.
b. Jason writes stories.
c. Newspapers give you information.

Questions

1. Who is a class news reporter?

2. What does he write stories about?

3. Who reads the stories?

- ❑ Talk about what you would write about if you were a class news reporter.
- ❑ Draw a picture or write about what you would write about if you were a class news reporter.

Practice Makes Perfect

Isabelle likes to play basketball. She is trying out for the girls' basketball team. Each day Isabelle and her dad practice dribbling and shooting goals. Her dad buys her a new pair of shoes for tryouts.

What is the main idea of this story?

a. Girls play basketball.

b. Isabelle practices for basketball tryouts.

c. Isabelle's dad buys her new shoes.

Questions

1. Who likes basketball?

2. What does she practice?

3. What does her dad buy her?

- ❏ Talk about a time you tried out for a sports team.
- ❏ Draw a picture or write about a time you tried out for a sports team.

Train Ride

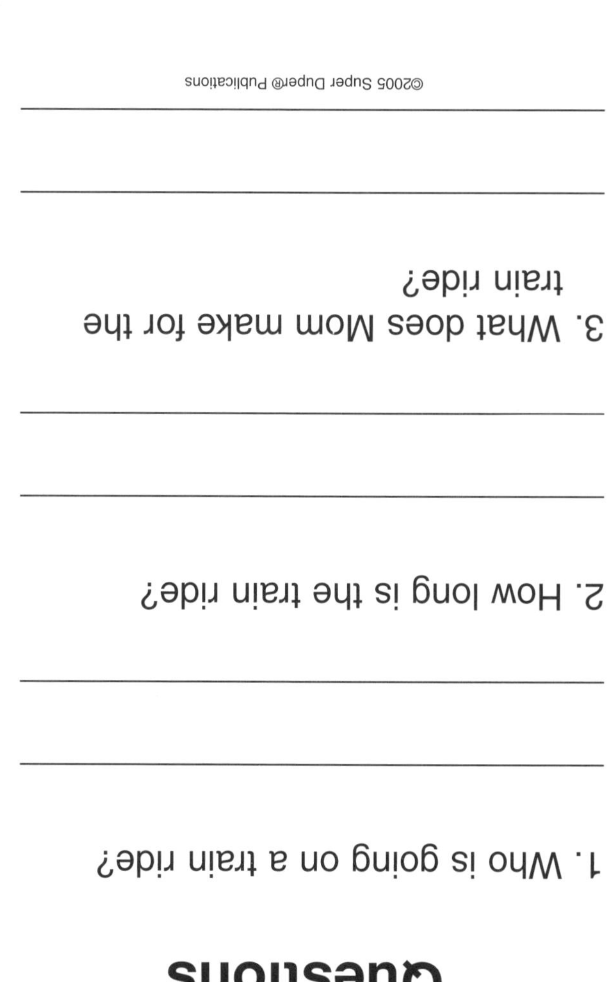

Amanda and Kevin are going to visit Grandma. They ride the train to Grandma's house. The train ride is one hour. Mom packed a lunch for them to eat on the train.

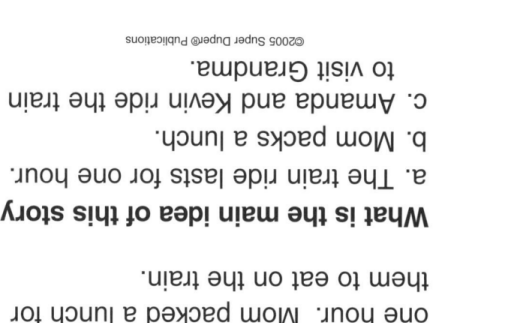

What is the main idea of this story?

a. The train ride lasts for one hour.
b. Mom packs a lunch.
c. Amanda and Kevin ride the train to visit Grandma.

Questions

1. Who is going on a train ride?

2. How long is the train ride?

3. What does Mom make for the train ride?

- ❏ Talk about who you would like to visit.
- ❏ Draw a picture or write about who you would like to visit.

Karate Time

Terrance is excited. Today is the first day of karate class. Terrance wears a white uniform to class. His neighbor, Harold, teaches the class.

What is the main idea of this story?

a. Terrance takes karate.
b. His neighbor is the teacher.
c. Karate is fun.

Questions

1. Who is excited?

____

____

2. What does he wear to class?

____

____

3. Who teaches the karate class?

____

____

❏ Talk about a sport you want to learn.

❏ Draw a picture or write about a sport you want to learn.

The Noise

Bill hears a noise coming from the bushes. He walks to the bushes to investigate the noise. He finds a bird nest with tiny blue birds chirping. He runs inside to tell his mom.

What is the main idea of this story?

a. Bill hears a noise.
b. Bill finds tiny blue birds in a nest.
c. Birds live in bushes.

1 2 3 4

Questions

1. Who hears a noise?

____

____

2. What is in the nest?

____

____

3. Who does he tell?

____

____

- ❑ Talk about a time you found a bird's nest.
- ❑ Draw a picture or write about a time you found a bird's nest.

Tree House

Brennan is building a tree house. He gathers small pieces of wood. He picks up his dad's ladder, hammer, and nails. Dad helps him hammer the pieces of wood together to build the tree house.

What is the main idea of this story?

a. Tree houses are made of wood.
b. Brennan likes to hammer.
c. Brennan and Dad are building a tree house.

Questions

1. Who is building a tree house?

____

____

2. What does he gather?

____

____

3. Who helps him hammer the wood together?

____

____

- ❑ Talk about something you want to build.
- ❑ Draw a picture or write about something you want to build.

Cut on dotted line

Piano Lessons

Holly quickly gets out of bed and gets dressed. Today she begins piano lessons. She has to be at her teacher's house at 9 a.m. Holly brings music sheets to the lesson.

What is the main idea of this story?

a. Holly begins piano lessons.
b. It is easy to play the piano.
c. Piano lessons are fun.

Questions

1. Who is this story about?

2. What time are the piano lessons?

3. What does she bring with her to class?

- ❑ Talk about a musical instrument you would like to play.
- ❑ Draw a picture or write about a musical instrument you would like to play.

Science Fair

Jamie is sitting at the kitchen table working on his science project. The science fair is Saturday. The winner will receive a trophy. Jamie really wants to win first place.

What is the main idea of this story?

a. Jamie is in the kitchen.

b. Jamie will participate in the science fair.

c. The winner gets a trophy.

Questions

1. Where is Jamie working?

____

____

2. What is he doing?

____

____

3. When is the science fair?

____

____

- ❑ Talk about a science fair project you have done.
- ❑ Draw a picture or write about a science fair project you have done.

Surprise Party

BK-323 Fold and Say® Auditory & Story Comprehension

Mrs. Maple has a surprise for her students. She decorates the classroom with balloons. The students eat chocolate cake and drink fruit punch. After the party, the students help Mrs. Maple clean the classroom.

What is the main idea of this story?

a. Mrs. Maple gives a surprise party for her students.
b. The students like cake.
c. Mrs. Maple is a good teacher.

Questions

1. Who is giving a surprise party?

____

____

2. What do the students eat?

____

____

3. What do they do after the party?

____

____

©2005 Super Duper® Publications

❑ Talk about a classroom party you have had.

❑ Draw a picture or write about a classroom party you have had.

Cut on dotted line

Cookout

It's a sunny afternoon. Mark invites his friends over to his house for a cookout. They cook hot dogs and hamburgers on the grill. Afterwards, they play football in the yard.

What is the main idea of this story?

a. Mark has a cookout.

b. Mark likes to eat hot dogs.

c. Sunny afternoons are fun.

Questions

1. Who does Mark invite to his house?

____

2. What do they grill?

____

3. What do they do after they eat?

____

- ❑ Talk about what you like to do at a cookout.
- ❑ Draw a picture or write about what you like to do at a cookout.

Cut on dotted line

Feeding the Monkeys

Carlos is at the zoo. He is watching the zookeeper feed lunch to the monkeys. The zookeeper gives the monkeys bananas. Carlos watches the monkeys peel and eat the bananas.

What is the main idea of this story?

a. Monkeys live in the zoo.
b. Monkeys are hungry.
c. Carlos watches the monkeys eat.

Questions

1. Who is at the zoo?

____

____

2. Who feeds the monkeys?

____

____

3. What do the monkeys eat?

____

____

- ❑ Talk about a time you saw animals being fed.
- ❑ Draw a picture or write about a time you saw animals being fed.

In a Hurry

Ramon wakes up late for school. He has five minutes before the bus picks him up. He puts on his clothes quickly. He grabs a banana for breakfast, as he runs out the door to get on the bus.

What is the main idea of this story?

a. Ramon likes bananas.
b. Ramon takes the bus to school.
c. Ramon is in a hurry.

Questions

1. Who wakes up late?

2. How long does he have until the bus picks him up?

3. What does he eat for breakfast?

- ❑ Talk about a time you were late for school.
- ❑ Draw a picture or write about a time you were late for school.

School Parade

Today is the school "crazy hat" parade. Everyone in my class decorates a hat to wear in the parade. Music plays as we walk down the street. We wave and clap our hands to the music.

What is the main idea of this story?

a. School parades have music.
b. You have to wear a hat to be in a parade.
c. My class is participating in the school "crazy hat" parade.

Questions

1. When is the school parade?

2. What does everyone wear in the parade?

3. What do they do when they hear the music?

- ❑ Talk about a time you were in a parade.
- ❑ Draw a picture or write about a time you were in a parade.

Too Early

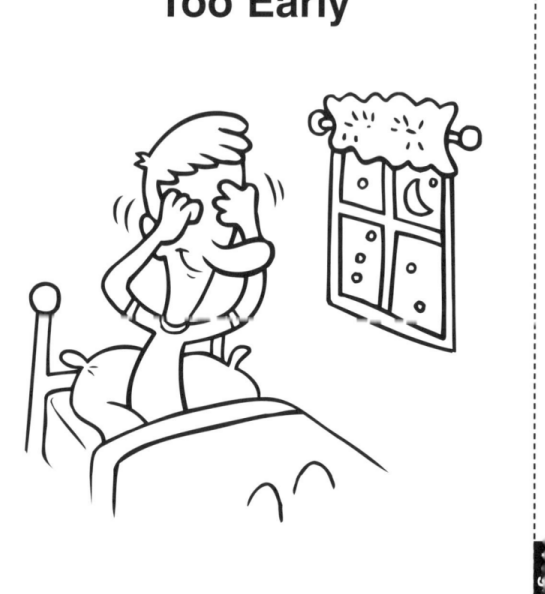

Rob rubbed his eyes as his alarm went off. He went downstairs to eat breakfast, but no one was up. He looked at the kitchen clock and realized it was midnight and not time to get up for school! He quickly ran upstairs and went back to bed.

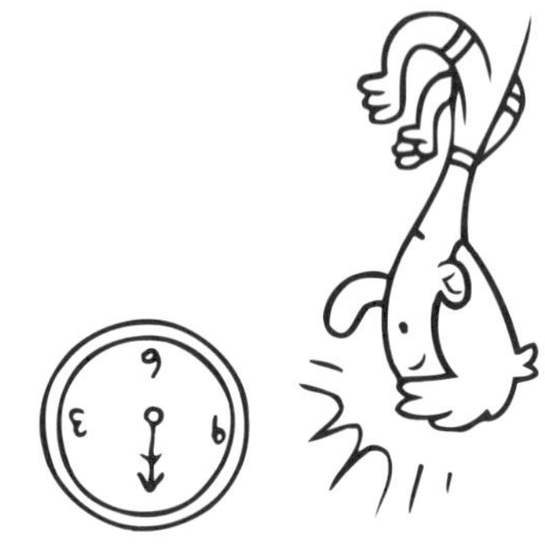

What is the main idea of this story?

a. Rob walks downstairs.

b. Rob's alarm went off too early.

c. Rob likes to eat breakfast.

Questions

1. Who is this story about?

2. What did he do after his alarm went off?

3. What did he do after he realized it wasn't time to go to school?

- ❏ Talk about a time you woke up during the night.
- ❏ Draw a picture or write about a time you woke up during the night.

Harriet Honeybee

Harriet Honeybee lives in a hive. She has an important job. She collects pollen from flowers on her hairy back legs. The pollen falls off and fertilizes other flowers.

What is the main idea of this story?

a. Honeybees spread pollen.

b. Honeybees can fly.

c. Honeybees are pretty.

Questions

1. Who collects pollen from flowers?

___

___

2. How does she carry the pollen?

___

___

3. What happens to the pollen?

___

___

- ❏ Talk about a time you have seen a bee.
- ❏ Draw a picture or write about a time you have seen a bee.

Ice Cream Cone

Melissa sits down on a park bench to eat her chocolate ice cream cone. She eats the ice cream cone before it melts. *Crunch!* This is the last bite!

What is the main idea of this story?

a. Melissa only likes chocolate ice cream cones.

b. Melissa is hungry.

c. Melissa eats an ice cream cone.

Questions

1. Who is this story about?

2. Where does she sit to eat her ice cream cone?

3. What flavor ice cream does she eat?

©2005 Super Duper® Publications

- ❏ Talk about your favorite ice cream cone.
- ❏ Draw a picture or write about your favorite ice cream cone.

Ant Farm

Mr. Lawson sets up an ant farm in the classroom. The students watch the ants work. They watch as the ants make tunnels through the ant farm to get from place to place. Soon, the ant farm is full of tunnels.

What is the main idea of this story?

a. The ants make tunnels.
b. Ants are small.
c. Mr. Lawson likes ants.

Questions

1. Who sets up the ant farm?

____

____

2. Who watches the ants work?

____

____

3. What do the ants make?

____

____

- ❑ Talk about a time you have seen ants.
- ❑ Draw a picture or write about a time you have seen ants.

Cut on dotted line

Level 2

The Move

The moving van pulls up in front of Eric's house. Eric sits on the steps holding his kitten, Murphy. The men take all the furniture and boxes out of Eric's house. Then, they climb into the van and drive to the new house.

What is the main idea of this story?

a. Eric likes kittens.
b. The men move Eric's furniture.
c. Eric is moving to a new house.

Questions

1. Who is moving?

____

____

2. What is he holding?

____

____

3. What do the men move out of his house?

____

____

- ❑ Talk about a time you have moved to someplace new.
- ❑ Draw a picture or write about a time you have moved to someplace new.

The Race

Steve is at the car race with Dad. He gets to see the cars racing around the track. His favorite race car on the track is blue. The blue car wins the race and the driver wins a trophy.

What is the main idea of this story?

a. Boys like race cars.
b. All race cars are blue.
c. Steve and Dad are at the car races.

Questions

1. Where is Steve?

____

____

2. What is his favorite color race car?

____

____

3. What does the winner receive?

____

____

❑ Talk about a time you saw a car race.

❑ Draw a picture or write about a time you saw a car race.

Cut on dotted line

Level 2

Winter Trip

Tye is having a hard time going to sleep. He is excited about going on a winter trip. Tye and his parents leave tomorrow morning. They will drive to the mountains to ski.

What is the main idea of this story?

a. Tye can't sleep.

b. Tye and his parents are going on a winter vacation.

c. Tye will leave tomorrow morning.

Questions

1. Who is having a hard time going to sleep?

____

____

2. When will they leave to go on the trip?

____

____

3. Where will they go?

____

____

- ❑ Talk about a time you were excited about a vacation.
- ❑ Draw a picture or write about a time you were excited about a vacation.

Cut on dotted line

Robbie Raccoon

Robbie Raccoon lives in the forest. He is a fast runner. He likes to run around the forest. He can run as fast as a bicycle!

What is the main idea of this story?

a. Robbie lives in the forest.
b. Robbie is a fast runner.
c. He likes to ride bicycles.

Questions

1. Who lives in the forest?

____

____

2. What can he do?

____

____

3. Where does he like to run?

____

____

- ❑ Talk about a time you saw a raccoon.
- ❑ Draw a picture or write about a time you saw a raccoon.

Sammy Snail

Sammy Snail is gray. He lives where it is moist and dark. He likes to be moist. When the weather gets too dry, Sammy buries himself in the wet ground to stay damp.

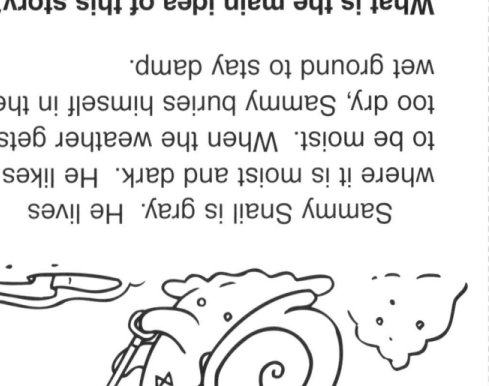

What is the main idea of this story?

a. Sammy Snail lives in a moist place.
b. Snails only eat plants.
c. Sammy Snail doesn't like the dry weather.

Questions

1. What color is Sammy?

2. Where does he live?

3. What does he do when the weather gets dry?

- ❏ Talk about a snail you have seen.
- ❏ Draw a picture or write about a snail you have seen.

Cut on dotted line

Tricks on Dad

Wendy can't wait for Dad to get home. She likes to play tricks on him. She hides his slippers under the kitchen table. She giggles as Dad looks for them.

What is the main idea of this story?

a. Wendy likes to giggle.
b. Dads wear slippers.
c. Wendy plays tricks on Dad.

Questions

1. Who is Wendy waiting for?

____

____

2. What does she hide?

____

____

3. Where does she hide them?

____

____

- ❏ Talk about a time you played a trick on someone.
- ❏ Draw a picture or write about a time you played a trick on someone.

Rafting Trip

Excitement is in the air as James and Dad reach the whitewater rafting camp. They are at camp for one week. They learn to ride a raft over the whitewater rapids. At night, they camp out on the riverbank.

What is the main idea of this story?

a. James and Dad are learning to whitewater raft.
b. James is excited.
c. They sleep on the riverbank.

Questions

1. Who is at camp?

2. How long will they be there?

3. What do they learn to do?

- ❑ Talk about a time you have been in a raft.
- ❑ Draw a picture or write about a time you have been in a raft.

Spelling Bee

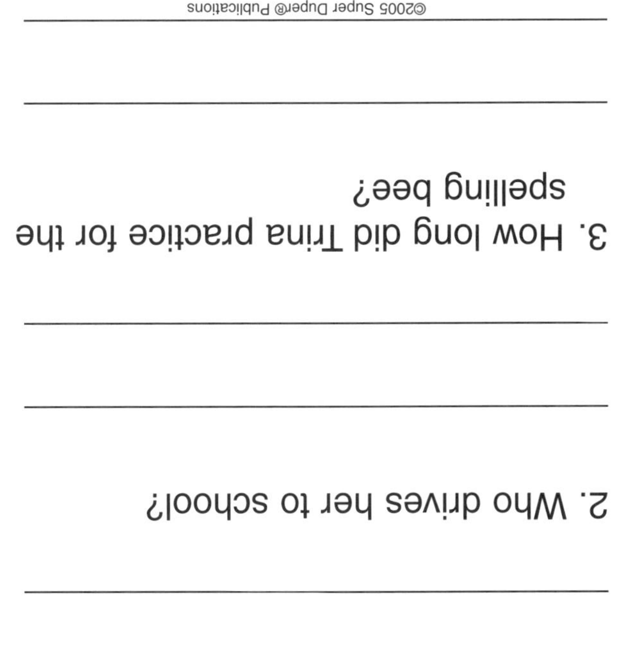

Trina is nervous as she gets dressed. Today is the spelling bee. Mom drives her to the school for the spelling bee. Trina has practiced spelling words every night for two months.

What is the main idea of this story?

a. Trina is getting dressed.

b. Trina is in a spelling bee.

c. All spelling bees are at school.

Questions

1. Who is nervous?

2. Who drives her to school?

3. How long did Trina practice for the spelling bee?

- ❏ Talk about a time you were nervous.
- ❏ Draw a picture or write about a time you were nervous.

Marty and the Coconuts

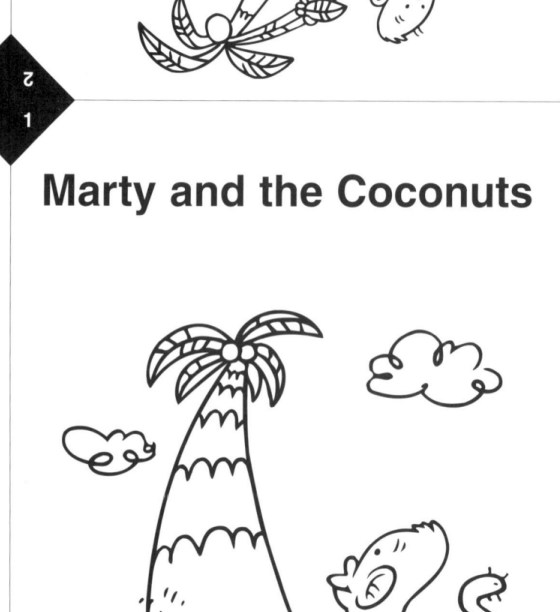

Marty Monkey looks up at the tall palm tree. He sees several coconuts at the top. He grabs a limb and swings until he reaches the top. He throws the coconuts down to the ground for his friends to eat.

What is the main idea of this story?

a. Marty is a monkey.

b. Marty gets coconuts from a tall tree.

c. Coconuts are good to eat.

Questions

1. What kind of animal is Marty?

2. How does he reach the top of the trees?

3. Who does he throw the coconuts to?

©2005 Super Duper® Publications

- ❏ Talk about a time you have seen monkeys at a zoo.
- ❏ Draw a picture or write about a time you have seen monkeys at a zoo.

Grandpa's Garden

Grandpa plants a garden every spring. He plants tomatoes and bell peppers. If it doesn't rain, he waters the garden. When the vegetables are ripe, he picks them and uses them to make sandwiches for lunch.

What is the main idea of this story?

a. Grandpa waters the garden.
b. Grandpa eats vegetables.
c. Grandpa has a garden.

Questions

1. Who plants a garden?

2. What does he plant?

3. What does he do when the vegetables are ripe?

- ❑ Talk about a time you planted a garden.
- ❑ Draw a picture or write about a time you planted a garden.

Charlie the Caveman

Charlie lives in a large cave on the side of a mountain. He hunts for food during the day. He cooks food over a fire. At night, he sleeps on a bearskin next to the fire.

What is the main idea of this story?

a. Charlie lives as a caveman.
b. Charlie sleeps next to the fire.
c. Only cavemen can build fires.

Questions

1. Where does Charlie live?

____

____

2. What does he do during the day?

____

____

3. What does he sleep on?

____

____

- ❏ Talk about what your cave would look like if you were a caveman or cavewoman.
- ❏ Draw a picture or write about what your cave would look like if you were a caveman or cavewoman.

Field Day

Kennedy is excited to go to school. Today is field day. There will be races and games for all the kids to play. Kennedy will run the 20-yard dash.

What is the main idea of this story?

a. Kennedy is a good runner.
b. Today is field day at Kennedy's school.
c. Races and games are fun.

Questions

1. Who is excited?

2. What is today?

3. What race will she run?

- ❏ Talk about a time you participated in field day.
- ❏ Draw a picture or write about a time you participated in field day.

Babysitter Fun

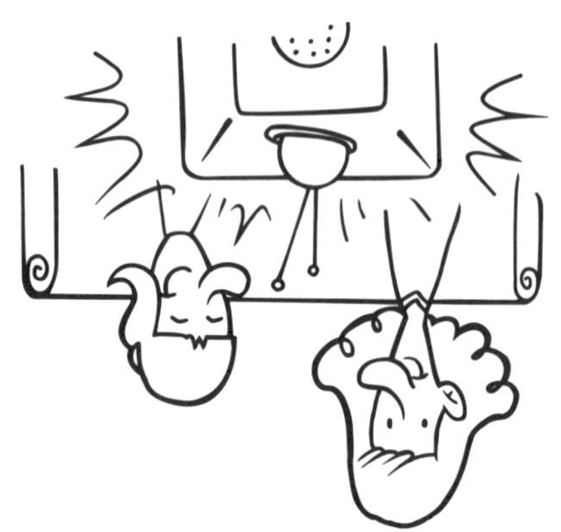

Anna's parents are going out to dinner tonight. Chelsea comes to babysit Anna. They make popcorn and watch movies. Anna goes to bed before her parents come home.

What is the main idea of this story?

a. Anna likes popcorn.
b. Anna and Chelsea watch TV.
c. Chelsea babysits Anna tonight.

Questions

1. Who is going out to dinner?

2. Who babysits?

3. What do they do?

- ❏ Talk about a time you had a babysitter.
- ❏ Draw a picture or write about a time you had a babysitter.

Justin's First Day

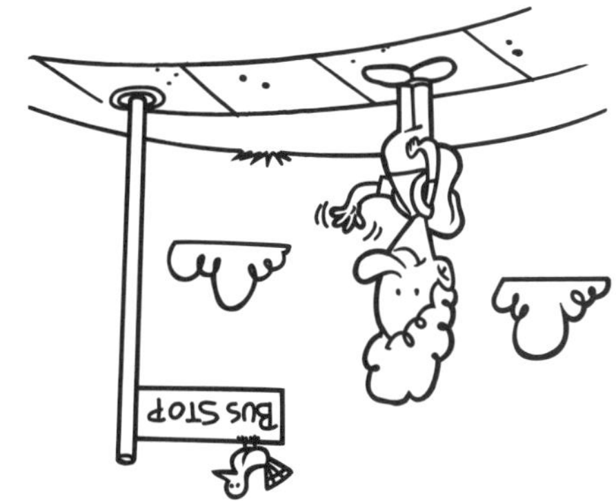

Today is the first day of school. Justin wakes up early and gets dressed. He puts on his new red backpack. He picks up his lunch bag and waits on the sidewalk for the school bus.

What is the main idea of this story?

a. Justin gets ready for school.
b. Justin has a new backpack.
c. Justin wakes up early.

Questions

1. Who wakes up early?

2. What color is his backpack?

3. Where does he wait for the school bus?

- ❏ Talk about your first day of school.
- ❏ Draw a picture or write about your first day of school.

Shopping with Mom

Sydney and Mom climb into the car. Mom drives to the mall. They shop all day for new clothes. Mom buys Sydney a new, pink dress.

What is the main idea of this story?

a. Mom drives a car.
b. Mom likes new dresses.
c. Sydney and Mom are shopping.

Questions

1. Who goes to the mall?

2. What do they shop for?

3. What does Mom buy?

- ❏ Talk about a time you went shopping with your parent or caregiver.
- ❏ Draw a picture or write about a time you went shopping with your parent or caregiver.

Level 2 Main Idea Answer Key

p. 64 Buried Treasure c
p. 65 Brian the Bullfrog c
p. 66 Best Friends ....b
p. 67 Danny Dragon c
p. 68 Mom's Birthday ....b
p. 69 The Tallest Animal ....a
p. 70 Calling 911 ....b
p. 71 The Ballerina ....b
p. 72 Lucy Ladybug......................c
p. 73 Cool Dad ....a
p. 74 Soccer Star ....a
p. 75 The Big Game c
p. 76 Leo's Pet c
p. 77 Tractor Rides ....b
p. 78 Lost Pet ....a
p. 79 The Artist c
p. 80 The Magic Carpet ....b
p. 81 Greg's Party ....a
p. 82 The Dude Ranch ....b
p. 83 Drive with Dad c
p. 84 Sleepy Alex ....a
p. 85 Beach Fun c
p. 86 Stella's Web ....b
p. 87 Super Detective c
p. 88 The Pumpkin c
p. 89 Melanie's Cookies ....a
p. 90 Birthday Present ....b
p. 91 Koala Bears c
p. 92 Message in a Bottle ....a
p. 93 Class News Reporter..........b
p. 94 Practice Makes Perfect ......b
p. 95 Train Ride............................c
p. 96 Karate Time ....a
p. 97 The Noise.........................b
p. 98 Tree House........................c
p. 99 Piano Lessons ....a
p. 100 Science Fair ....b
p. 101 Surprise Party ....a
p. 102 Cookout ....a
p. 103 Feeding the Monkeys........c
p. 104 In a Hurry c
p. 105 School Parade c
p. 106 Too Early ....b
p. 107 Harriet Honeybee..............a
p. 108 Ice Cream Cone................c
p. 109 Ant Farm ....a
p. 110 The Move c
p. 111 The Race c
p. 112 Winter Trip ....b
p. 113 Robbie Raccoon................b
p. 114 Sammy Snail ....a
p. 115 Tricks on Dad c
p. 116 Rafting Trip ....a
p. 117 Spelling Bee......................b
p. 118 Marty and the Coconuts....b
p. 119 Grandpa's Garden c
p. 120 Charlie the Caveman ....a
p. 121 Field Day ....b
p. 122 Babysitter Fun c
p. 123 Justin's First Day ....a
p. 124 Shopping with Mom c

Your ______________ skills are

Out of Sight!

____
Awarded To

____
Presented By

____
Date

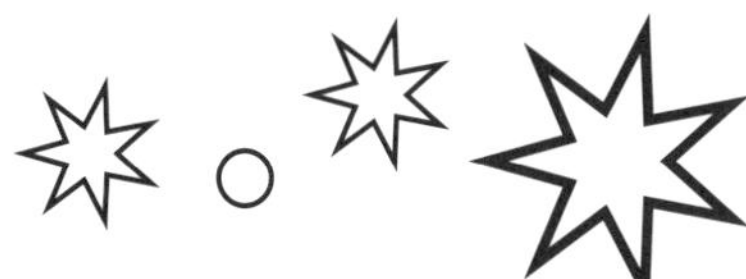
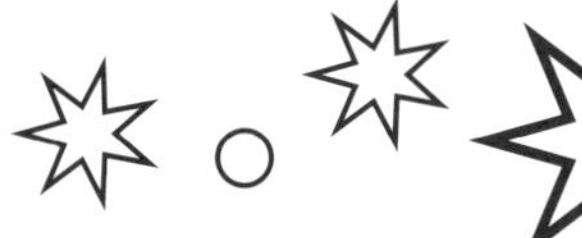
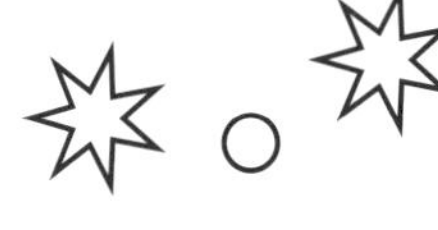

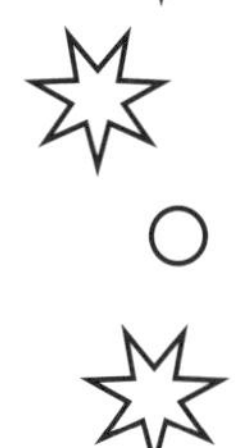

Student's Name

is a Main Idea Magician!

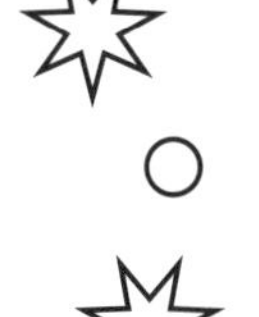

Awarded By

Date

Way To Go!

____

Student's Name

has improved ______________ **skills!**

______________________________ ______________

Awarded By Date

Auditory Adventures® Activities Pack

Laminated Open-Ended, Token, Barrier, Bingo, & Lotto Games for Auditory Association, Discrimination, Memory, and Reception

Grades PreK-5

by Kim Gill, Joanne DiNinno, Ashley Drennan, Thomas Webber

This is the best listening activity kit anywhere! It addresses 21 specific auditory skills.

You receive 18 awesome laminated games for one to six players.

- Eight open-ended games (11˝ x 17˝).
- Auditory Bingo and Listening Lotto game, in a set of six each (8½˝°x 11˝).
- Two barrier games, in sets of six (8½˝ x 11˝).
- Four open-ended chip/token games, in sets of six (8½˝ x 11˝).
- Two targeted listening games, in sets of six.
- Provides an easy-to-follow, 180-page Lesson Activity Book with instant auditory activities and reproducible homework sheets.
- Includes six packs of crayons, over 200 tokens (6 colors), and a die.
- Comes in a long-lasting, water-resistant tote

Ask for item ....#GB-654
Auditory Adventures® Activities Pack

Say and Do® Auditory Lessons

Grades Pre K-5

by Diane Hyde

Improve your students' auditory processing skills at two skill levels, beginner and advanced, with this 60-page reproducible. Lesson sheets target twenty areas of listening development.

Ask for item ....#BK-313
Say and Do® Auditory Lessons

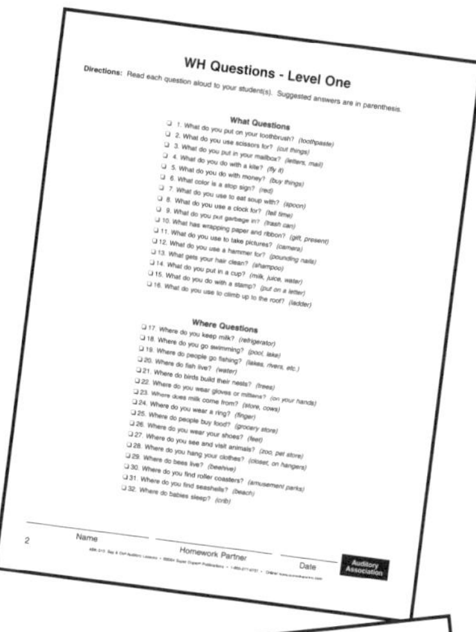

WH Questions - Level One

Directions: Read each question aloud to your student(s). Suggested answers are in parenthesis.

What Questions

- ❑ 1. What do you put on your toothbrush? *(toothpaste)*
- ❑ 2. What do you use scissors for? *(cut things)*
- ❑ 3. What do you put in your mailbox? *(letters, mail)*
- ❑ 4. What do you do with a kite? *(fly it)*
- ❑ 5. What do you do with money? *(buy things)*
- ❑ 6. What color is a stop sign? *(red)*
- ❑ 7. What do you use to eat soup with? *(spoon)*
- ❑ 8. What do you use a clock for? *(tell time)*
- ❑ 9. What do you put garbage in? *(trash can)*
- ❑ 10. What has wrapping paper and ribbon? *(gift, present)*
- ❑ 11. What do you use to take pictures? *(camera)*
- ❑ 12. What do you use a hammer for? *(pounding nails)*
- ❑ 13. What gets your hair clean? *(shampoo)*
- ❑ 14. What do you put in a cup? *(milk, juice, water)*
- ❑ 15. What do you do with a stamp? *(put on a letter)*
- ❑ 16. What do you use to climb up to the roof? *(ladder)*

Where Questions

- ❑ 17. Where do you keep milk? *(refrigerator)*
- ❑ 18. Where do you go swimming? *(pool, lake)*
- ❑ 19. Where do people go fishing? *(lakes, rivers, etc.)*
- ❑ 20. Where do fish live? *(water)*
- ❑ 21. Where do birds build their nests? *(trees)*
- ❑ 22. Where do you wear gloves or mittens? *(on your hands)*
- ❑ 23. Where does milk come from? *(store, cows)*
- ❑ 24. Where do you wear a ring? *(finger)*
- ❑ 25. Where do people buy food? *(grocery store)*
- ❑ 26. Where do you wear your shoes? *(feet)*
- ❑ 27. Where do you see and visit animals? *(zoo, pet store)*
- ❑ 28. Where do you hang your clothes? *(closet, on hangers)*
- ❑ 29. Where do bees live? *(beehive)*
- ❑ 30. Where do you find roller coasters? *(amusement parks)*
- ❑ 31. Where do you find seashells? *(beach)*
- ❑ 32. Where do babies sleep? *(crib)*

2 Name ______ Homework Partner ______ Date ______ Auditory Association

WH Questions - Level Two

Directions: Read each question aloud to your student(s). Suggested answers are in parentheses.

When Questions

- ❑ 1. When do you eat dinner? *(at night)*
- ❑ 2. When do you brush your teeth? *(morning, night, after a meal)*
- ❑ 3. When do you see sunshine? *(during the day)*
- ❑ 4. When do trees grow new leaves? *(in the spring)*
- ❑ 5. When do you eat breakfast? *(in the morning)*
- ❑ 6. When do you go swimming outside? *(in the summer)*
- ❑ 7. When do you see the moon? *(at night)*
- ❑ 8. When do you see a rainbow? *(after it rains)*
- ❑ 9. When do the leaves fall from the trees? *(in the fall)*
- ❑ 10. When does a bear sleep for a long time? *(winter)*
- ❑ 11. When does a rooster crow? *(in the morning)*
- ❑ 12. When do flowers bloom? *(in the spring)*
- ❑ 13. When do bats fly? *(night)*
- ❑ 14. When do you sleep? *(night)*
- ❑ 15. When do you see icicles? *(in the winter)*

Why Questions

- ❑ 16. Why do leaves fall from trees? *(the leaves are dead, change of seasons)*
- ❑ 17. Why do you use an eraser? *(to fix a mistake)*
- ❑ 18. Why do you brush your teeth? *(to keep them clean, so you won't get cavities)*
- ❑ 19. Why do you use an umbrella? *(so you won't get wet)*
- ❑ 20. Why do you wear shoes? *(to protect your feet)*
- ❑ 21. Why do you use suntan lotion? *(so you won't get burned)*
- ❑ 22. Why do you wear a seat belt? *(to protect you in case of an accident)*
- ❑ 23. Why do you put gas in a car? *(to make it run)*
- ❑ 24. Why do we go to sleep? *(our bodies need to rest)*
- ❑ 25. Why do you use soap? *(to clean things)*
- ❑ 26. Why do children go to school? *(to learn)*
- ❑ 27. Why do people wear eyeglasses? *(so they can see better)*
- ❑ 28. Why do football players wear helmets? *(to protect their heads)*
- ❑ 29. Why do people drive cars? *(to get from place to place)*
- ❑ 30. Why do you water flowers? *(so they will grow, so they won't die)*

4 Name ______ Homework Partner ______ Date ______ Auditory Association

MagneTalk® Match-up Adventures Kit

Language-Based Magnetic Barrier Games and Activities

Grades PreK-5

by Jeanne Goodwin & Audrey Prince

This one of a kind magnetic masterpiece targets a ton of language and listening skills. It targets:

- Following Directions
- Deductive Reasoning
- Giving Directions
- Vocabulary
- Auditory Memory
- Storytelling
- Basic Concepts
- Categorization
- Rhyming
- Listening

The Magnetalk® Adventures Kit includes 10 gorgeous game boards (two of each scene: Camping, Picnic, Outer Space, Ocean, and Grocery Store). A 12" x 16" two-sided magnetic/dry erase tabletop easle. Ten magnets for each game board (100 magnetic pieces), and a 34 page reproducible activity book with a CD-ROM for easy printing.

Ask for item................................#GB-181
MagneTalk® Match-up Adventures Kit

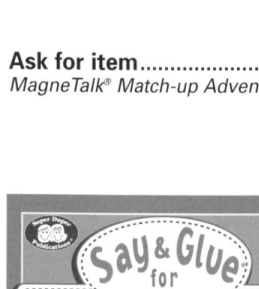

Say & Glue® for Language & Listening

Fun Sheets!

Grades PreK-3

by Alyson D. Price

Your students will be in cut-and-paste heaven while they listen and learn to categorize, tell what items are used for, follow directions, retell stories, and understand basic concepts (25 in all). Each of the 94 two-part activities have:

- A full-page picture scene with terrific artwork.
- An activity page with 4-12 directions to follow, 3-5 language expansion activities (*Name something a bird does*), and cut and paste pictures.

Ask for item..#BK-307
Say & Glue® for Language & Listening

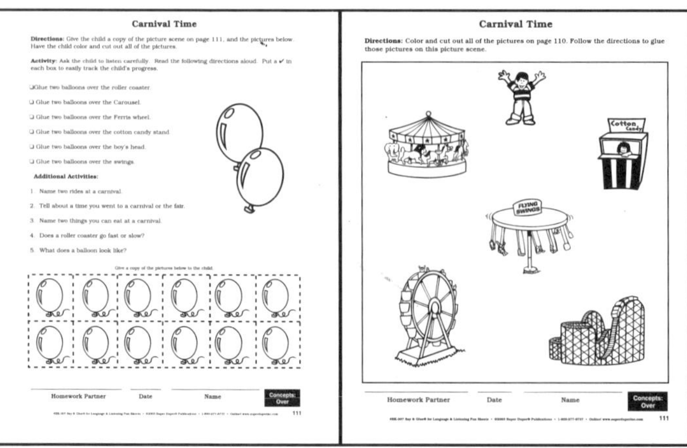

Carnival Time

Directions: Give the child a copy of the picture scene on page 111, and the pictures below. Have the child color and cut out all of the pictures.

Activity: Ask the child to listen carefully. Read the following directions aloud. Put a ✔ in each box to easily track the child's progress.

- ❑ Glue two balloons over the roller coaster.
- ❑ Glue two balloons over the Carousel.
- ❑ Glue two balloons over the Ferris wheel.
- ❑ Glue two balloons over the cotton candy stand.
- ❑ Glue two balloons over the boy's head.
- ❑ Glue two balloons over the swings.

Additional Activities:

1. Name two rides at a carnival.
2. Tell about a time you went to a carnival or the fair.
3. Name two things you can eat at a carnival.
4. Does a roller coaster go fast or slow?
5. What does a balloon look like?

Give a copy of the pictures below to the child.

Homework Partner Date Name Concepts: Over

Carnival Time

Directions: Color and cut out all of the pictures on page 110. Follow the directions to glue those pictures on this picture scene.

Cotton Candy

Flying Swings

Homework Partner Date Name Concepts: Over